W9-ABJ-335

DATE DUE

APR 11 2013	
	PRINTED IN U.S.A.

TRAILBLAZERS
IN SCIENCE AND TECHNOLOGY

Luc Montagnier

IDENTIFYING THE AIDS VIRUS

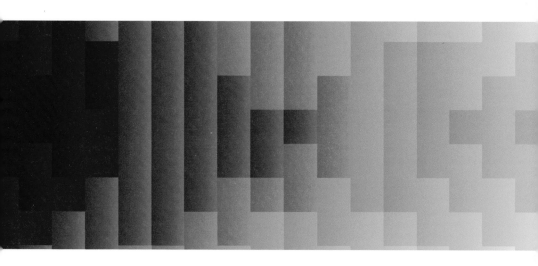

TRAILBLAZERS
IN SCIENCE AND TECHNOLOGY

Luc
Montagnier

IDENTIFYING THE AIDS VIRUS

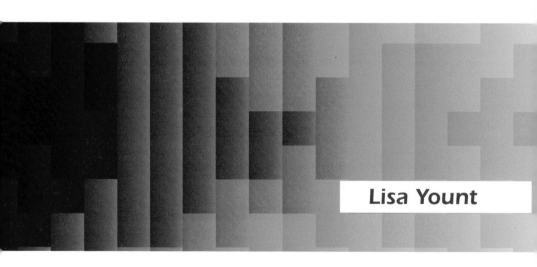

Lisa Yount

CHELSEA HOUSE
An Infobase Learning Company

LUC MONTAGNIER: Identifying the AIDS Virus

Chelsea House
An imprint of Infobase Learning
132 West 31st Street
New York NY 10001

Library of Congress Cataloging-in-Publication Data

Yount, Lisa.
  Luc Montagnier : identifying the AIDS virus / Lisa Yount.
      p. cm. — (Trailblazers in science and technology)
  Includes bibliographical references and index.
  ISBN 978-1-60413-661-6
  1. Montagnier, Luc—Juvenile literature. 2. HIV (Viruses)—Juvenile literature. 3. AIDS (Disease)—Juvenile literature. I. Title. II. Series.
  QR414.6.H58Y68 2011
  616.97'9201—dc22   2010047006

Chelsea House books are available at special discounts when purchased in bulk quantities for businesses, associations, institutions, or sales promotions. Please call our Special Sales Department in New York at (212) 967-8800 or (800) 322-8755.

You can find Chelsea House on the World Wide Web at http://www.infobaselearning.com

Text design by Erika K. Arroyo
Composition by Hermitage Publishing Services
Illustrations by Bobbi McCutcheon
Photo research by Suzanne M. Tibor
Cover printed by Bang Printing, Brainerd, Minn.
Book printed and bound by Bang Printing, Brainerd, Minn.
Date printed: October 2011
Printed in the United States of America

10 9 8 7 6 5 4 3 2 1

This book is printed on acid-free paper.

To Tom and Debbie, going through their own disasters

Contents

Preface

Trailblazers in Science and Technology is a multivolume set of biographies for young adults that profiles 10 individuals or small groups who were trailblazers in science—in other words, those who made discoveries that greatly broadened human knowledge and sometimes changed society or saved many lives. In addition to describing those discoveries and their effects, the books explore the qualities that made these people trailblazers, the personal relationships they formed, and the way those relationships interacted with their scientific work.

What does it take to be a trailblazer, in science or any other field of human endeavor?

First, a trailblazer must have imagination: the power to envision a path where others see only expanses of jungle, desert, or swamp. Helen Taussig, Alfred Blalock, and Vivien Thomas imagined an operation that could help children whose condition everyone else thought was hopeless. Louis and Mary Leakey looked at shards of bone embedded in the rocks of an African valley and pictured in them the story of humanity's birth.

Imagination alone will not blaze a trail, however. A trailblazer must also have determination and courage, the will to keep on trudging and swinging a metaphorical machete long after others fall by the wayside. Pierre and Marie Curie stirred their witch's cauldron for day after day in a dirty shed, melting down tons of rock to extract a tiny sample of a strange new element. The women astronomers who assisted Edward Pickering patiently counted and compared white spots on thousands of photographs in order to map the universe.

Because their vision is so different from that of others, trailblazers often are not popular. They may find themselves isolated even from those who are working toward the same goals, as Rosalind Franklin did in her research on DNA. Other researchers may brand them as outsiders and therefore ignore their work, as mathematicians did at first with Edward Lorenz's writings on chaos theory because Lorenz's background was in meteorology (weather science), a quite different scientific discipline. Society may regard them as eccentric or worse, as happened to electricity pioneer Nikola Tesla and, to a lesser extent, genome analyst and entrepreneur Craig Venter. This separateness sometimes freed and sometimes hindered these individuals' creative paths.

On the other hand, the relationships that trailblazers do form often sustain them and enrich their work. In addition to supplying emotional and intellectual support, compatible partners of whatever type can build on one another's ideas to achieve insights that neither would have been likely to develop alone. Two married couples described in this set, the Curies and the Leakeys, not only helped each other in their scientific efforts but inspired some of their children to continue on their path. Other partnerships, such as the one between Larry Page and Sergey Brin, the computer scientists-turned-entrepreneurs who founded the Internet giant Google, related strictly to business, but they were just as essential to the partners' success.

Even relationships that have an unhealthy side may prove to offer unexpected benefits. Pickering hired women such as Williamina Fleming to be his astronomical "computers" because he could pay them far less than he would have had to give men for the same work. Similarly, Alfred Blalock took advantage of Vivien Thomas's limited work choices as an African American to keep Thomas at his command in the surgical laboratory. At the same time, these instances of exploitation, so typical of the society of the times, gave the "exploited" opportunities that they would not otherwise have had. Thomas would not have contributed to lifesaving surgeries if he had remained a carpenter in Nashville, even though he might have earned more money than he did by working for Blalock. Fleming surely would never have discovered her talent for astronomy if Pickering had kept her as merely his "Scottish maid."

Competitors can form almost as close a relationship as cooperative partners, and like the irritating grain of sand in an oyster's shell that eventually yields a pearl, rivalries can inspire scientific trailblazers to heights of achievement that they might not have attained if they had worked unopposed. Tesla's competition with Thomas Edison to establish a grid of electrical power around U.S. cities stimulated as well as infuriated both men. Venter's announcement that he would produce a readout of humanity's genes sooner than the massive, government-funded Human Genome Project (HGP) pushed him, as well as his rival, HGP leader Francis Collins, to greater efforts. The French virologist Luc Montagnier was spurred to refine and prove his suspicions about the virus he thought was linked to AIDS because he knew that Robert Gallo, a similar researcher in another country, was close to publishing the same conclusions.

It is our hope that the biographies in the Trailblazers in Science and Technology set will inspire young people not only to discover and nurture the trailblazer within themselves but also to trust their imagination, even when it shows them a path that others say cannot exist, yet at the same time hold it to strict standards of proof. We hope they will form supportive relationships with others who share their vision, yet will also be willing to learn from those they compete with or even dislike. Above all, we hope they will feel the curiosity about the natural world and the determination to unravel its secrets that all trailblazers of science share.

Acknowledgments

I would like to thank Frank K. Darmstadt for his help and suggestions, Suzie Tibor for her hard work in rounding up the photographs, Bobbi McCutcheon for the outstanding line art, my cats for keeping me company (helpfully or otherwise), and, as always, my husband, Harry Henderson, for—well—everything.

Introduction

Infectious diseases—those caused by microorganisms—have been a dreaded part of life since humankind's beginning. Those that are *contagious,* or capable of being transmitted from person to person, could sweep through cities or countries like a forest fire, producing *epidemics* that infect or even kill a high percentage of the inhabitants.

Many infectious diseases are as old as human history, but once in a while, even in modern times, a seemingly new epidemic disease appears. Because only a few cases of such an illness are usually reported at first, busy scientists—let alone the government agencies and private organizations that fund scientific research—may not recognize the threat that the disease presents. The risk of neglect is especially great if the disease seems to strike only groups that a society's mainstream shuns. Research to discover the illness's cause and treatment may begin in earnest only when the epidemic starts to spread into the society as a whole.

ANGLING FOR A "BIG FISH"

Research on the disease later known as *AIDS (acquired immunodeficiency syndrome)* followed this path. The illness, first reported among homosexual men in the United States in 1981, attracted little notice in its early years. One scientist who did pay attention to it was Luc Montagnier (1932–   ), a French expert on *viruses.* These microorganisms, so tiny that they are visible only under electron microscopes, are considered to be on the border between living and nonliving things because they can reproduce only inside living cells. Viruses had been shown to cause many epidemic diseases, including influenza (flu) and smallpox, and Montagnier suspected that a virus would prove to cause the new ailment as well.

Luc Montagnier, shown here in his laboratory, won the Nobel Prize in physiology or medicine in 2008 for his discovery of HIV (human immunodeficiency virus), the virus that causes the deadly disease AIDS (acquired immune deficiency syndrome). *(Service photographie/Institut Pasteur)*

Montagnier was well aware of how frustrating the search for a new virus could be. Certain viruses had been shown to cause cancer in animals, and, along with a number of other researchers in the 1970s, he had believed that viruses might play a role in at least some human cancers as well. He had hunted for such viruses for years without success. He wrote in his autobiography, *Virus:*

> The day-to-day life of researchers consists mostly of disappointments, with the occasional success that allows them to maintain their enthusiasm. One must have the mentality of a gambler or fisherman. As for me, I am only interested in big fish. But they are rather rare.

Montagnier thought that the virus that caused the new disease might prove to be a very "big fish" indeed—if he could capture it.

At the start of 1983, Montagnier and two other scientists working with him at the Institut Pasteur in Paris, Jean-Claude Chermann (1939–   ) and Françoise Sinoussi (1947–   , later Barré-Sinoussi), began searching for viruses in a tissue sample taken from a man in the early stages of the mystery disease. They quickly discovered a virus and found evidence that it might be new to science.

INTERNATIONAL DISPUTES

As Montagnier's group worked to learn more about their virus, they collaborated at first with Robert Gallo (1937–   ), a U.S. scientist who was also looking for a virus that might prove to be the cause of AIDS. Collaboration gave way to rivalry, however, when Gallo began isolating viruses of his own. The rivalry intensified after Margaret Heckler (1931–   ), secretary of the U.S. Department of Health and Human Services, announced at a news conference in April 1984 that Gallo had found the AIDS virus and made little mention of the French team's work.

What had been chiefly a personal feud between Montagnier and Gallo took on international dimensions in the mid-1980s, when the institutes for which the two scientists worked, and the government agencies that in turn sponsored the institutes, dueled over the right to patent the tests that the groups had developed to reveal signs of infection in samples of blood. The test patent was bound to be worth millions of dollars because AIDS had been shown to be transmitted partly through blood, so the world's supplies of banked blood needed to be screened to prevent the spread of the disease through transfusions.

The governments of the United States and France officially settled the issue in 1987, dividing both scientific credit and income from the test patent equally. Resentments continued to simmer, however, and important scientific questions remained unanswered. Genetic analysis showed that the viruses Montagnier and Gallo had used to develop their blood tests were virtually identical—a seemingly amazing coincidence because the genes of the virus, by then known as *HIV (human immunodeficiency virus),* had proved to change, or *mutate,* so easily that the *genomes* (complete collections of genes) of viruses isolated from different patients (or even the same patient at different times) often differed by 5 or 10 percent. Montagnier had shared samples of his virus with Gallo in late 1983, and some journalists suggested that Gallo might have deliberately "stolen" the French virus and claimed it as his own. Further research finally explained the mystery in 1991, revealing that a fast-growing strain of the French virus had contaminated cultures in Gallo's laboratory without either group's knowledge.

"Competition [in science] is good—it stimulates fields," Robert Gallo told National Institutes of Health historian Victoria Harding in 1995. The competition between Montagnier and Gallo, each spurring the other on, may have been one of the reasons why the cause of AIDS was identified so quickly—within three years of the first published report of the disease. On the other hand, their painful rivalry, intensified by politics and media attention, distracted these two vital investigators at a time when the AIDS epidemic was spreading rapidly through the world and learning more about the virus that caused it was crucial. The conflict also provided a disturbing public display of the all-too-human side of science.

AIDS continues to take a deadly toll of the world's population, but Luc Montagnier is still fighting to stop it. As head of the World Foundation for AIDS Research and Prevention, he has played a major part in efforts to minimize the social and personal effects that AIDS has had on the countries that the epidemic has hit hardest, especially those in Africa. He has also continued his research on HIV and made several significant discoveries about the virus and its effects on the body. Along with one of his team members, Françoise Barré-Sinoussi, Montagnier won a share of the Nobel Prize in physiology or medicine in 2008—the crowning honor among the many he has earned as the discoverer of HIV and one of the chief researchers who cast light on the terrible disease it causes.

A STELLAR CAREER

This volume of the Trailblazers of Science and Technology set describes Luc Montagnier's life and career, including his pioneering early work on viruses and cancer, his laboratory's discovery of HIV, his complex relationship with fellow virologist Robert Gallo, and his later research on AIDS and attempts to reduce the impact of the AIDS epidemic. Chapter 1 covers Montagnier's youth and early research, including his discovery of a new way to grow cancer cells in the laboratory.

Chapter 2 describes the start of the AIDS epidemic and explains how Montagnier became involved in the hunt for the cause of the mysterious disease. Chapter 3 chronicles the Montagnier laboratory's isolation of HIV and the difficulties the group experienced in trying to make scientists and government officials in the United States and France pay attention to their work. Robert Gallo's isolation of a similar virus and research linking it to AIDS, as well as his increasingly tense relationship with Montagnier, are the subjects of chapter 4.

Chapter 5 recounts the international struggle for scientific credit and the legal battle for patent rights to the AIDS blood test that came to overshadow the work of both Montagnier and Gallo during the mid-1980s. An agreement signed by no less than the president of the United States and the premier of France was supposed to end these disputes in 1987, but, as chapter 6 explains, bad feelings and scientific questions remained. New investigations in the early 1990s finally resolved those issues. This chapter also describes Luc Montagnier's later research, his work as the head of an international AIDS charity, and the many honors he won for his achievements, culminating in the Nobel Prize in 2008. The book concludes with an overview of the worldwide AIDS epidemic today and the hopes that Montagnier and others have for someday bringing this scourge to an end.

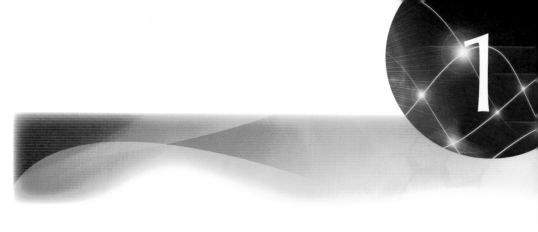

Learning about Viruses

Luc Montagnier's parents grew used to surprises coming out of their basement when their son was a teenager. Antoine and Marianne Montagnier knew that these little shocks, ranging from strange smells to the occasional bang of a small explosion, were merely the side effects of Luc's chemistry experiments. They could hardly complain: Luc, after all, was following in his father's footsteps. Antoine Montagnier earned his living as a certified public accountant, but science was one of his hobbies. Earlier, when Luc was a boy, Antoine had conducted his own chemical and electrical experiments on weekends.

AN UNCERTAIN CHILDHOOD

Occasional explosions were nothing compared to some of the early events in Luc's life. He was born on August 18, 1932, in Chabris, France, a town south of Tours, and spent his childhood in the village of Grand-Pont, near "the ancient boundary between northern and southern France," as he wrote in his autobiography, *Virus.* Tragedies could occur even in this quiet countryside, and one struck the Montagnier family in 1937, when Luc was five years old. He ran into the street without looking, and a speeding car struck him. To make matters worse, the impact threw him into a patch of broken glass left from a previous accident, producing cuts all over his face and body. For two days he lay in a coma, his survival uncertain, and then awoke with no

1

memory of the crash. He recovered completely except for a few scars on his face.

Two years later, Luc's family faced a longer-lasting challenge. During World War II (1939–45), Germany seized control of France. The Montagniers moved to nearby Châtellerault, where Luc and other children learned to read in an unheated schoolroom. Like other families, the Montagniers had little to eat—"nothing . . . but potatoes and bread," *Chicago Tribune* reporter John Crewdson quoted Montagnier as saying in Crewdson's book about the discovery of the AIDS virus, *Science Fictions.* According to Crewdson, Montagnier believed that this malnutrition, occurring at a key time in his growth, made him shorter than average.

The Allies (Britain, the United States, the Soviet Union, and other countries opposing the Germans) bombed parts of France in an attempt to drive the Germans out. One of these bombs destroyed part of the Montagniers' home in June 1944, fortunately without injuring either Luc or his parents. After the war ended with Germany's defeat, the town gave the Montagniers a house formerly occupied by the Gestapo, the greatly feared German secret police. Luc suspected that the chemistry experiments he later conducted there, explosions and all, were harmless compared to the "sinister purpose" for which the Germans might have used the basement.

FIRST RESEARCH

Amateur scientist though Antoine Montagnier was, he and his wife nonetheless hoped that Luc would study literature and then law, eventually entering his father's profession. Luc, however, remained focused on science as he approached college age. His grades in the high school in Châtellerault were not good enough to obtain admission to a college program that emphasized physical sciences, so he turned instead to biology, which he saw (he wrote later in *Virus*) as "the next best thing." He also became interested in medicine after seeing his grandfather die a slow, painful death from bowel cancer. Luc's thoughts about studying to be a physician led his parents to hope that he would become a respected family doctor in Châtellerault, but Luc knew from the beginning that he wanted to pursue research rather than treating patients.

When he was 17, Luc Montagnier entered the University of Poitiers, which was near his home. He took both premedical courses and classes in "natural sciences," as biology was called at the time. He spent his mornings in training at the city hospital, his afternoons in science classes, and his evenings listening to lectures on anatomy, the study of the body's structure.

This school, more like what would now be called a junior college than a full-fledged university, offered only two years of rather limited training. Few of its professors knew much beyond basic science. One exception was Montagnier's professor of botany (the study of plants), Pierre Gavaudan, who was (Montagnier wrote in his autobiography) a "passionate master of research." Under his influence, Montagnier began to see biology as more than a second choice. The young man even started doing research of his own, combining a microscope and a movie camera to film microorganisms in the water of ponds near the university.

One subject of Montagnier's films was an alga, or water plant, called mesocarpus. Like the cells of most other plants, those of mesocarpus contain the green pigment chlorophyll, which helps plants convert energy from sunlight into nourishment. The chlorophyll in this alga is located in a small body termed a chromatophore. Montagnier's movies showed that when sunlight shone strongly on the alga's cells, the chromatophores turned their edges toward the light. When the light was weaker, on the other hand, the chromatophores rotated inside the cells to expose as much of their surface to it as possible. These movements allowed the chromatophores to keep the amount of sunlight they received fairly constant.

A few other scientists had noticed this phenomenon, but its details were poorly understood. Montagnier used colored filters to reveal that the blue, rather than the red, part of sunlight triggers the movement, even though chlorophyll absorbs only red light. This meant that other pigments in the cell had to be involved in the chromatophore's reaction. Montagnier's films also showed that movement in the *cytoplasm,* the jellylike material that fills the main part of the cell, turned the chromatophore. This study, Montagnier's first independent research work, helped to earn him a bachelor's degree in natural science from the University of Poitiers in 1953.

VIRUSES AND CELLS

Luc Montagnier continued his medical and scientific training in Paris. He soon found himself neglecting his medical school classes in order to go on with his own research, which now focused on certain kinds of bacteria. He completed his training and earned his M.D. degree, but he decided not to compete for an internship (a postgraduate hospital position for young doctors) because working in a hospital would take too much time away from his science studies.

In 1955, just after Montagnier had received his advanced degree (licentiate) in science from the University of Paris, Pierre Gavaudan, Montagnier's former professor at Poitiers, introduced him to another professor who worked at the Institut Curie. (This well-known cancer research center in Paris was named after its founder, famed physicist and chemist Marie Curie [1867–1934].) This professor needed an assistant, and Montagnier needed a paying research position, so the two joined forces, and Montagnier became an assistant in cellular biology at the institute. He also taught physiology (the study of the functions of different parts of the body) at the Sorbonne, another highly respected Paris university.

At the Institut Curie, the professor's research turned Montagnier's interest from plant to animal cells. Montagnier also began studying certain viruses that live in these cells, in particular the virus that causes foot-and-mouth disease, a highly contagious and sometimes-fatal disease of cattle, sheep, and other hoofed animals. Viruses, the tiniest known microorganisms, are many times smaller than bacteria. Scientists had first proposed their existence in the last years of the 19th century, but they are too small to be visible under a microscope that uses light. Researchers therefore were able to observe them directly only after electron microscopes were invented in the 1930s. Because viruses can reproduce only when they are inside cells, they are considered to be on the border between living and nonliving things.

In addition to *virology,* or the study of viruses, Montagnier also began learning about *molecular biology,* a then-new branch of science that investigates biological processes by studying the structure and function of the complex molecules in the bodies of living things. The greatest advance in that field had been made in 1953, when a young researcher from the United States, James Dewey Watson (1928–   ), and a somewhat older British scientist, Francis Harry Compton Crick (1916–2004), worked together at Britain's prestigious Cambridge University to discover the molecular structure of *deoxyribonucleic acid (DNA),* a substance in the *nucleus,* or central body, of cells. Experiments in the 1940s and early 1950s had provided evidence that DNA is the carrier of the inherited information, passing it along during reproduction of cells and organisms. DNA encodes the instructions that tell cells how to make *proteins,* the large group of biochemicals that does most of the work in cells.

By the time Montagnier began studying virology, researchers had learned that viruses consist of DNA or a related chemical, *ribonucleic acid (RNA),* surrounded by a protein coat. Research teams in the United States and Germany

James Watson *(left)* and Francis Crick worked out the molecular structure of deoxyribonucleic acid (DNA), the substance that transmits inherited (genetic) information in most living things. They are shown here in 1953, the year of their discovery, with their model of part of the molecule. *(A. Barrington Brown/Photo Researchers, Inc.)*

had shown independently in the mid-1950s that only the RNA in tobacco mosaic virus, a common virus that causes a disease in tobacco plants, is necessary for the virus to reproduce and trigger the illness. This was the first demonstration that RNA, like DNA, could carry genetic information.

The virus Montagnier was studying, the foot-and-mouth disease virus, also contains RNA. Montagnier and Jean Leclerc, another researcher in the Institut Curie laboratory, tried to extract this RNA from cells that the virus had infected. In the process, Montagnier developed a new method for

(continues on page 8)

DNA: THE SECRET OF HEREDITY

James Watson and Francis Crick not only discovered the structure of DNA molecules but also showed how that structure allows the molecules to reproduce themselves, which they must do in order to pass on the information they contain each time a cell divides. Crick and other researchers went on to reveal how cells use the instructions coded into DNA to make proteins.

Each molecule of DNA is made up of two long strands of alternating smaller molecules—sugars and phosphates. (A phosphate is a compound containing the element phosphorus.) Pairs of other molecules called *bases*, joined by hydrogen bonds, extend between the long strands like the rungs of a ladder. There are four kinds of bases, represented by the letters G, C, T, and A. G always pairs with C, and T always pairs with A. The "ladder" twists around and around to form a long coil, or *helix*.

The hydrogen bonds at the center of the DNA helix are weak and break open easily. When a cell prepares to divide, it signals the bonds to release their grip, and the DNA molecule comes apart lengthwise like a zipper unzipping. Each base on the two single strands attracts its pair-mate from free-floating chemicals in the nucleus, and the hydrogen bonds re-form. The result is two identical DNA molecules where only one had existed before. Because of this duplication, each of the "daughter cells" produced when the cell splits in two receives a copy of all the DNA molecules that make up the cell's genome, or complete collection of genes.

The information in DNA is coded into the order, or sequence, of bases in the DNA molecule. A *gene* is a stretch of DNA whose sequence carries the code for making a single protein or, sometimes, performing another function such as controlling another gene. When a cell needs to make a protein, it copies the sequence of the gene carrying that protein's information into a molecule of DNA's chemical cousin, ribonucleic acid (RNA), creating an RNA molecule with essentially the same sequence.

DNA cannot leave the cell's nucleus, but RNA can. The new RNA molecule travels from the nucleus into the cytoplasm, where small molecules called *amino acids* attach themselves to the RNA in an order specified by the sequence of bases in the RNA molecule. The amino acid molecules then link together like beads on a necklace to form the protein.

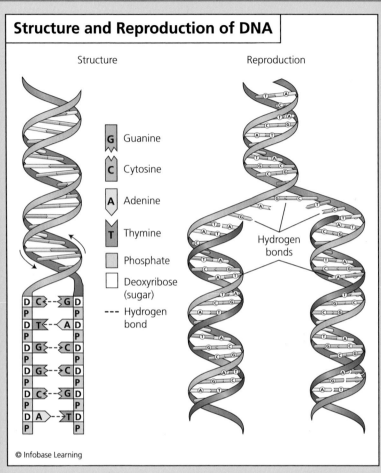

Structure and Reproduction of DNA

Structure

Reproduction

G Guanine

C Cytosine

A Adenine

T Thymine

Phosphate

Deoxyribose (sugar)

--- Hydrogen bond

Hydrogen bonds

© Infobase Learning

Watson and Crick found out that the structure of the DNA molecule allows it to encode genetic information and to reproduce itself so that the information can be passed on to both daughter cells when a cell divides. The molecule has a helix (coil or corkscrew) shape, in which two "backbones" of alternating deoxyribose (a sugar) and phosphate (a compound containing phosphorus) molecules twine around one another. Pairs of small molecules called bases, joined by hydrogen bonds, stretch between the backbones like the rungs of a twisted ladder. Genetic information is encoded in the order, or sequence, of the bases. When the DNA molecule reproduces, the hydrogen bonds break down and the molecule comes apart lengthwise like a zipper unzipping. Each of the four kinds of bases (represented by the letters A, G, C, and T) can pair with only one other kind of base. The bases in the single strands attract their pair-mates and more "backbone" molecules from free-floating molecules in the cell, reassembling two double strands identical to the original one.

(continued from page 5)
increasing the amount of viral RNA that penetrated into the cells. This work helped him earn a doctorate in medicine from the University of Paris in 1960.

VIRUS REPRODUCTION

Luc Montagnier felt that his opportunities to learn further scientific skills were limited in France. Many French scientists, including the professor in charge of his laboratory, seemed to know little about the techniques of molecular biology, for instance. He therefore decided to do his postdoctoral research outside the country. In 1960, he became a researcher with the Centre National de la Recherche Scientifique (CNRS), the French government's chief research institute. Then, as part of a scientific exchange program between this agency and its equivalent in Britain, the Medical Research Council (MRC), he obtained a scholarship to work with British researcher Kingsley Sanders at the MRC laboratory in Carshalton, a suburb of south London.

Montagnier left for Britain in July 1960. Since his English was limited to a few phrases learned in a quick summer school course before his departure, he was thrilled to find that Sanders spoke perfect French. The laboratory also contained several other French researchers. During his first few days in England, Montagnier also met Dorothea Ackerman, a young woman who became his wife the following year. They later had three children.

Sanders's laboratory, which Montagnier's autobiography called "one of the best in virology" at the time, was studying a RNA virus that causes a fatal disease in mice. Montagnier decided to learn more about how this virus reproduces.

By that time, scientists knew the basic mechanism by which viruses reproduce. The process begins when a virus particle attaches itself to proteins on the surface of a cell. The virus injects its genetic material (DNA or RNA) into the cell like a tiny hypodermic needle, leaving its protein coat behind. The genetic material then takes over the cell's gene-copying machinery and forces it to reproduce the virus's genes instead. The cell produces a host of new viruses, complete with protein coats. The viruses break out of the cell, usually destroying it, and go on to infect other cells. Beyond this general knowledge, however, the details of the reproduction were unclear.

After three years of hard work, often occupying weekends as well as weekdays, Montagnier proved that during the reproduction of this RNA virus, the single-stranded molecule of viral RNA becomes a two-stranded helix similar to the shape that Watson and Crick had shown DNA molecules to possess. Montagnier and Sanders described this discovery in an article in the highly regarded science magazine *Nature* in 1963. The finding was important because it showed that RNA could reproduce on its own by base pairing, just as DNA could.

GROWING CANCER CELLS

Partly because of the groundbreaking work that Sanders had done with Montagnier, the Memorial Sloan-Kettering Cancer Center in New York offered Sanders a research position, and he accepted. The Carshalton laboratory team dissolved after his departure. Montagnier moved to a new institute of virology that was part of the University of Glasgow (Scotland), "a haven of modernity and warmth" (he wrote in *Virus*) in that industrial city.

Michael Stoker and Ian MacPherson, the heads of the laboratory in which Montagnier was to work, were studying viruses that cause cancer in animals. Researchers had known since the early 20th century that certain viruses could have this effect. Peyton Rous (1879–1970), a scientist at the Rockefeller Institute (later Rockefeller University) in New York, showed in 1911 that a type of cancer in chickens could be transmitted by injections of ground-up tumor material that had been passed through filters fine enough to screen out the tiniest bacteria. He therefore concluded that a virus must cause this form of cancer. Many scientists refused to accept his idea until electron microscopes revealed the virus, which came to be known as *Rous sarcoma virus,* for the first time in 1947.

Researchers identified several other types of cancer-causing virus in the late 1930s and 1940s. Stoker and MacPherson were studying one of these, called polyoma ("many tumors") virus, which can produce a variety of tumors in hamsters and other small animals. Working with MacPherson and Italian scientist Renato Dulbecco (1914–   ) in 1964, Montagnier developed a way to grow hamster cells made cancerous by the virus in a jellylike nutrient medium known as *agar,* which is made from seaweed. Laboratory researchers frequently raised colonies of bacteria in flat dishes filled with agar, but no one had grown cancer cells in it before. Normal hamster cells did not grow in the agar, so researchers using the new technique could tell whether the virus had changed cells into a cancerous form without having to inject the cells into animals and wait to see whether they grew into tumors. Applying Montagnier's discovery, the Glasgow team showed that pure DNA from the polyoma virus could turn normal cells into cancerous ones—yet another proof that DNA is the carrier of genetic information. Montagnier's technique soon became the standard method for growing cancer cells in laboratory colonies, or *cultures*.

"BACKWARDS" VIRUSES

Luc Montagnier returned to France later in 1964 and began working at the Institut Curie once more. From 1965 to 1972, he was director of a laboratory at the institute's facility in Orsay, a suburb of Paris. He wanted to continue his study of cancer-causing viruses, especially the Rous sarcoma virus, and use his agar technique to try to identify viruses able to cause cancer in humans. No such virus had yet been identified, but Montagnier hoped that he would be the first to find one. He could not make cells taken from fresh human tumors thrive in the agar medium, however.

By this time, researchers were beginning to realize that Rous sarcoma virus and other RNA-containing viruses that cause cancer are special. They not only force cells to copy their genetic material, like other viruses, but somehow change the cells' own genomes, resulting in cancer. In 1965, Montagnier and two other researchers showed that by treating polyoma virus with high-energy radiation, which altered the virus's genes in random ways, they could separate its power to infect (enter) cells and reproduce in them from its ability to produce cancer. Even after radiation had made the viruses unable to reproduce, they could still make cells cancerous when put into them. This suggested that the viruses contained a cancer-causing gene that was separate from the genes it needed for reproduction.

No one yet knew exactly how these unusual viruses reproduce. Montagnier believed that they formed double strands of RNA, like the virus he had studied in Carshalton. Another scientist, Howard Temin (1934–94) of the University of Wisconsin, Madison, had a different idea, however. Temin insisted that the viruses could copy their RNA into a DNA molecule with the same sequence of bases as that in the RNA. They then insert this DNA into the DNA of the cell's genome. Every time that cell reproduces, Temin theorized, it copies the genes of the virus along with its own and passes those genes on to the new cells, potentially creating new viruses.

(*opposite page*) (1) When a retrovirus infects a cell, only the virus's genetic material (in the form of RNA) enters the cell; the virus's protein coat remains outside. (2) Using a unique enzyme called reverse transcriptase, the virus's RNA copies its sequence of bases into DNA. It inserts this DNA into the host cell's genome as a provirus, forcing the cell to make proteins that the new viruses will need. (3) When the cell reproduces its DNA before dividing, it reproduces the provirus along with the rest of the genome. Both daughter cells resulting from the cell division therefore will carry proviruses.

Most scientists did not accept Temin's idea at first because researchers generally believed that DNA could copy itself into RNA but not the reverse. In 1970, however, Temin and David Baltimore (1938–   ), then at the

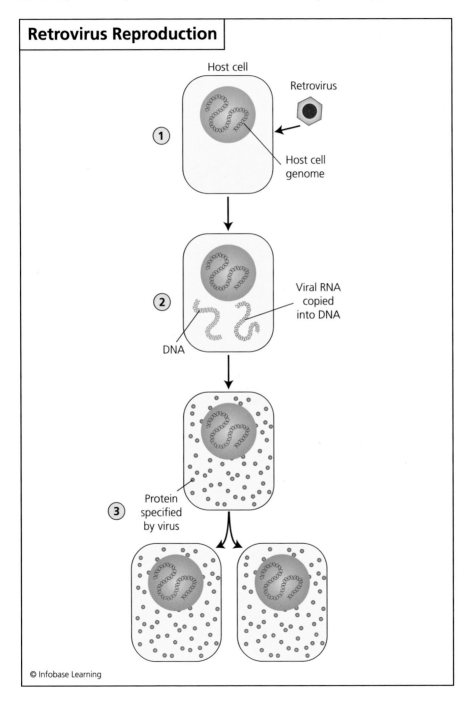

Retrovirus Reproduction

Host cell

Retrovirus

Host cell
genome

1

Viral RNA
copied
into DNA

2

DNA

Protein
3   specified
by virus

© Infobase Learning

Massachusetts Institute of Technology, independently discovered an enzyme called *reverse transcriptase,* which allows RNA to be copied into DNA. (*Enzymes* are a large group of proteins that speed up chemical reactions or make them possible.) RNA viruses that use reverse transcriptase to reproduce their genetic material became known as *retroviruses,* or "backwards viruses," because their copying mechanism is the reverse of the usual one.

MOVE TO THE INSTITUT PASTEUR

By the start of the 1970s, Luc Montagnier was becoming restless. He felt that his work at the Institut Curie was not moving forward as much as he would have wished, but he was not sure where else to go. Then, in 1971, he met

Luc Montagnier joined the Institut Pasteur in Paris, shown here, in 1972. A bust of the institute's founder, the famed French chemist Louis Pasteur (1822–95), is in front of the institute's main building. *(Institut Pasteur)*

Jacques Monod (1910–76), the head of Paris's famed Institut Pasteur, and several of the scientists who worked there. Louis Pasteur (1822–95), a chemist who became an expert on microorganisms and one of France's best-known scientists in the late 19th century, had founded the institute in 1888.

Montagnier liked the "Pasteurians," and he began to think about transferring to the institute. Monod asked him to do so in November. The older scientist told Montagnier that he planned to reorganize the institute's virology department, and he offered Montagnier the directorship of a laboratory within it. Montagnier was happy to accept. He helped Monod plan the Institut Pasteur's new viral oncology (the study of cancer's relationship to viruses) unit and became its head in 1972. He also won an award for his previous work, the Prix Rosen de Cancérologie, in the same year.

Montagnier's laboratory was one of many that were studying cancer-causing viruses at the time. After reverse transcriptase was discovered, these viruses had become a very popular research topic. Scientists had identified viruses that could produce cancer in monkeys and apes, close evolutionary relatives of humans, and they had shown that cancer-causing retroviruses could be transferred from one species to another. Many researchers therefore were sure that viruses capable of causing cancer in people must also exist. Some even thought that most or all human cancer would prove to be due to viruses.

In the early 1970s, scientists at different laboratories around the world raced to be the first to discover a virus that could produce cancer in humans. They felt sure that such a virus, if it existed, would be a retrovirus, just like the viruses that cause cancer in animals. The most efficient way to spot such viruses, some scientists believed, would be to test samples of human cancers for the presence of reverse transcriptase. Only retroviruses make this enzyme, so finding it in cancer cells would provide indirect evidence that the cells contained a retrovirus, even if the virus could not be seen under an electron microscope.

RESEARCH ON INTERFERON

Luc Montagnier continued searching for human retroviruses, but his research soon took on an additional subject us well. He focused on a substance called *interferon,* which cells make after viruses infect them. This messenger molecule instructs nearby healthy cells to make biochemicals that can stop the viruses from multiplying.

The body produces only tiny amounts of interferon, and scientists did not know how to make it artificially. Montagnier hoped to increase the amount of interferon available for study by means of *genetic engineering,* a technique that two California scientists developed in 1973. Genetic engineering allows genes to be transferred from one species to another.

Most genes carry the blueprints for making proteins. If a scientist inserts a gene containing the code for a particular protein into a bacterium, that bacterium begins making the protein, even though it would never do so in its natural state. The bacterium also passes on the inserted gene along with its own genes each time it reproduces—which bacteria do several times each hour. In just a day or so, a researcher can create a large colony of bacteria that are all exact copies, or *clones,* of a single engineered bacterium. The cloned bacteria act as "factories" to make large amounts of the protein for which the inserted gene carries the code. In reproducing, they also make numerous copies of the gene itself, which allows scientists to study it more easily.

Montagnier hoped to make interferon in this way. At first he expected the extra interferon to be used only for research, but in the long term, he and some other researchers thought that interferon might be made into a medication or vaccine against viruses. Interferon also indirectly slows the multiplication of cells and had reduced the growth of cancer cells in laboratory experiments, so the scientists hoped it might prove to be a new treatment for human cancer as well.

Not everyone welcomed genetic engineering, however. That technology was in its infancy in the mid-1970s, and many members of the public—as well as some scientists—feared that it might present unknown dangers. They were concerned that genetically engineered bacteria might escape from laboratories and cause epidemics of untreatable disease, for example. To ease these fears, scientists in the United States agreed in 1974 to do genetic engineering research on disease-causing microorganisms only in laboratories that had been specially constructed to make the escape of microbes almost impossible.

Scientists in most European countries, including France, quickly decided to follow the standards that the U.S. scientists had established. Institut Pasteur constructed a high-safety laboratory, which the institute scientists nicknamed "the submarine" because it was as hard to enter and leave as an undersea vessel. Because they did not yet have the technology to transfer a human interferon gene into bacteria, Montagnier's team had to search through numerous bacterial colonies in the hope of finding one that made the protein naturally—a process that Montagnier's autobiography says was "like looking for a needle in a haystack." Some of the bacteria they checked were able to cause disease, so the researchers had to do their work in the "submarine." A team in Switzerland later succeeded in finding bacteria that made interferon and went on to manufacture it by cloning the bacteria, but it proved disappointing as an anticancer drug.

CANCER-CAUSING GENES

In the early 1970s, while Luc Montagnier was investigating interferon, Peter Duesberg (1936–   ) of the University of California, Berkeley, and other scientists made a major discovery about the Rous sarcoma virus. A form of the virus that could not cause cancer proved to differ from the normal, cancer-causing form by only a single gene, which the harmless form lacked and the cancer-causing form possessed. The researchers named the gene *src*, for sarcoma, the type of cancer that this virus produces. Other scientists soon found different *oncogenes*, or cancer-causing genes, in other viruses that produce tumors in animals. Genes very similar to oncogenes were also discovered in healthy, noncancerous cells. Since retroviruses reproduce by inserting their genes into a cell's genome, researchers thought at first that ancient retroviruses had inserted these *proviruses*, as they were called, into cell genomes long ago. The proviruses then had been passed on, in a harmless form, as cells and organisms multiplied. Only when gene-damaging agents such as radiation or certain chemicals made the genes mutate did the proviruses become active and able to cause cancer once more.

Michael Bishop (1936–   ) and Harold Varmus (1939–   ), two scientists at the University of California, San Francisco, turned this idea on its head in 1976. They showed that the cellular, or provirus, form of *src* in fact was not a viral gene at all but a normal chicken gene involved in cell growth and reproduction. Rather than inserting the potentially deadly gene into the chicken genome, the Rous sarcoma virus apparently had taken up the gene from the chicken cells during its own reproduction at some time in its evolutionary past. Within the virus, the gene had mutated into a deadly form that the virus then passed on, producing cancer in the cells it infected.

After this key discovery, many cancer researchers turned their attention from viruses to oncogenes. Other oncogenes first found in cancer-causing viruses also proved to be mutated forms of normal genes that spur or regulate cell growth. The race to identify cancer-causing viruses was replaced by a race to identify cancer-causing genes. During the next few years, scientists in Bishop and Varmus's laboratory and others found normal forms of oncogenes in a wide variety of species, including humans.

LONELY VIRUS HUNTERS

Excitement about oncogenes was not the only reason that research on human cancer viruses lagged in the late 1970s. Scientists in the field were disillusioned because every claim to have found such a virus so far had proved to be a false alarm. Most of the mistakes could be traced to one of two problems. First, although normal cells do not produce reverse transcriptase, they do make a group of similar enzymes called DNA polymerases. It was easy to mistake one of these compounds for reverse transcriptase. Second, laboratories often studied animal cancer viruses at the same time they searched for viruses that could infect humans, and the animal viruses sometimes accidentally contaminated the plates or test tubes containing cultures of human cells. Researchers then spotted the viruses and announced that they had finally glimpsed their elusive prey, only to learn after closer inspection that they had been wrong. Because of these errors, many researchers came to doubt that viruses that could cause cancer in humans existed.

Luc Montagnier was one of the few scientists who continued to hunt for viruses that might play a role in human cancer. He thought that human retroviruses might have been hard to find because interferon blocked virus reproduction even more effectively in humans than it did in animals. He knew that by injecting a small amount of interferon into animals, certain scientists had made the animals' *immune systems* (the body's defense system) produce molecules called *antibodies* that destroyed interferon, just as injecting a small amount of killed viruses or bacteria in a vaccine makes the immune system create antibodies that will destroy live viruses or bacteria of the same type. The antibodies float in the *serum,* or clear (cell-free) part of the blood, which can be harvested from the animal. Several scientists, including some in Montagnier's own laboratory, had shown that injecting anti-interferon serum into animals with a retrovirus infection made the infection worse. Montagnier hoped that he could use the same substance to increase the amount of possible human retroviruses in cell cultures, thus improving the chances of detecting such a virus.

Montagnier and two other scientists in his laboratory, Jean-Claude Chermann and Françoise Sinoussi, set out to test his idea in 1977. They showed that anti–interferon serum increased the production of retrovirus in infected mouse cells by 10 to 50 times. They then began experiments on cancer cells from human victims of *leukemia,* a cancer affecting immune system cells (sometimes called *white cells*) in the blood. Unfortunately, even with the help of the anti-interferon, they failed to isolate any viruses from their human cultures. They also searched for viruses in human breast cancers, but this effort failed as well.

Robert Gallo (1937–   ), a researcher at the National Cancer Institute (NCI) in the United States, was another persistent virus hunter. The NCI is part of the National Institutes of Health (NIH), a large research complex in Bethesda, Maryland, that is sponsored by the U.S. government. Gallo had faced his share of frustrations, including an instance of contamination that had forced him to withdraw a previous claim of finding a human retrovirus, but in 1979 his determination was finally rewarded. Bernard Poiesz, a researcher in Gallo's laboratory, identified what appeared to be a new retrovirus in a patient with a rare form of cancer in which the abnormal cells were

Robert Gallo of the U.S. National Cancer Institute, shown here, discovered the first virus shown to cause cancer in humans, HTLV-1, and played an important part in showing that the virus later called HIV causes AIDS. He and Luc Montagnier have sometimes collaborated and sometimes competed. *(Institute of Human Virology, University of Maryland School of Medicine)*

T cells, a type of white cell that comes from the thymus (a gland in the neck). Sensitized by their earlier embarrassment, Gallo and his team conducted more than a year's worth of tests to make sure that no known viruses had contaminated their cells before announcing their discovery. Their first paper describing the virus, which Gallo called *HTLV-1 (human T-cell leukemia virus 1),* appeared in the *Proceedings of the National Academy of Sciences* in December 1980. A group of Japanese scientists independently found what proved to be the same virus at about the same time and linked the virus to several cases of a rare form of leukemia in southern Japan.

START OF A COLLABORATION

After learning about the discovery of HTLV-1, Luc Montagnier sent Gallo (whom he had first met in 1973) the results of his anti-interferon experiments, and the two began a collaboration. Françoise Sinoussi took some anti-interferon serum to the United States to see whether it would increase the production of a monkey retrovirus that had infected a culture of human cells in Gallo's laboratory. The substance worked, though not as well as it had done for the French. Two scientists on Gallo's team had discovered a growth factor, later known as *interleukin-2,* which allowed normal T cells to be grown in laboratory cultures for the first time, and Gallo in turn shared some of this factor with Montagnier. Montagnier hoped that combining interleukin-2 with anti-interferon serum would encourage possible human retroviruses to grow more vigorously in cell cultures, making identification and study of the viruses easier.

Gallo's laboratory discovered a second, related human retrovirus, which they called HTLV-2, in early 1981. They also learned much more about HTLV-1. They and other researchers found that this retrovirus could be transmitted by sexual contact and infected blood. Mothers could also pass the virus to their children at or before birth. HTLV-1 proved to be responsible for clusters of disease cases, not only in Japan, but in the Caribbean and parts of sub-Saharan Africa as well. In addition to causing cancer, it sometimes made people susceptible to infections from other microorganisms that are normally harmless, which suggested that it damaged the patients' immune systems. All these features would soon come to sound eerily familiar to both Montagnier and Gallo as they turned their attention to a new and far more widespread plague.

A Mysterious Epidemic

Michael Gottlieb was bewildered. A physician friend, knowing that Gottlieb was interested in conditions that reduce the function of the immune system, had urged the young researcher to visit room 516 of the hospital attached to the University of California, Los Angeles (UCLA), the institution that sponsored Gottlieb's own work. On October 6, 1980, Gottlieb took his friend's advice—and was shocked by what he saw. The 31-year-old man in the hospital bed had a serious infection of his mouth and esophagus (the tube that leads from the mouth to the digestive system) caused by fungus, a plantlike microorganism. Gottlieb knew that only people whose immune systems had been damaged, for instance by anticancer medications or drugs that keep the body from rejecting transplanted organs, developed this kind of infection. This man was not taking any such drugs. Neither the man's doctors nor Gottlieb could find any reason why the man's bodily defense system should be so weak.

Analysis of the patient's blood confirmed an immune system problem: Most of the man's white cells seemed to be missing. Researchers in those days were just beginning to devise tests that could identify particular kinds of white cells, and Gottlieb happened to know one of the few people who could carry out such a test. He asked his fellow scientist for help, and the man performed the test for him. The results revealed that the missing cells were a type of T cell termed *CD4 lymphocytes*. (A *lymphocyte* is a cell that circulates in the *lymph system,* a set of glands and vessels separate from, but

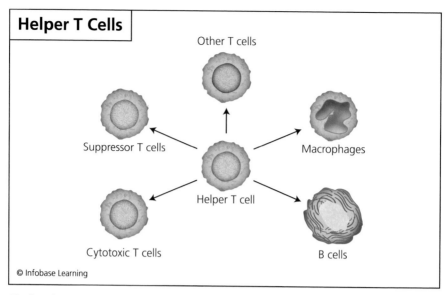

Helper T Cells

Other T cells

Suppressor T cells

Macrophages

Helper T cell

Cytotoxic T cells

B cells

© Infobase Learning

CD4 lymphocytes, also called helper T cells, produce chemical signals that activate several other kinds of immune system cells when an infection occurs. Once activated, macrophages devour bacteria; B cells produce antibodies that attach to foreign proteins and mark them for destruction; cytotoxic T cells kill cells that have been infected with viruses; and suppressor T cells turn off the production of antibodies after the infection has been controlled. Once the AIDS virus destroys most of the body's helper T cells, the other cells cannot function, and opportunistic infections invade the body.

connected to, the blood system. The lymph system is part of the immune system. Lymphocytes can travel in the blood as well as in the *lymph,* the clear fluid carried in the vessels of the lymph system.) These cells, sometimes called *helper T cells,* direct the activities of most other cells in the immune system. When they detect bacteria or viruses, they send out chemical signals that activate several other types of cells. Those cells, in turn, destroy the invaders. Without CD4 lymphocytes, the immune system is helpless, even though other types of white cells might still be present.

STRANGE INFECTIONS

Medication cleared up the sick man's fungus infection, but a few days later he was back in the hospital. This time he had a dry, hacking cough and a fever, and he was so tired that he could hardly walk. The cough became worse, developing into a lung disease called *pneumonia,* which threatened the man's ability to breathe. Michael Gottlieb realized that unless the doctors learned quickly what microorganism was causing the pneumonia and treated it with an appropriate antibiotic, the man was likely to die.

Remembering a few unusual cases of pneumonia that he had seen in the hospital at nearby Stanford University, Gottlieb suspected that this man's illness was not produced by the bacteria that usually cause such problems. He sent samples of fluid and tissue from the patient's lungs to the laboratory, and tests there confirmed his guess: The microorganisms behind the infection were parasites called *Pneumocystis carinii.* Gottlieb knew that pneumocystis itself is common, but, like the fungus that had attacked the man earlier, it seldom causes disease because healthy immune systems easily destroy it.

Gottlieb had only one clue that might help him guess why the young man's immune system was failing to do its job: The man admitted to being homosexual, or "gay," the slang term. He was one of many gay men who had finally rebelled against the prejudices that forced them to keep their sexual orientation secret. During the 1970s, such men had flocked to a few large American cities—notably San Francisco, Los Angeles, New York, and Miami—and established colonies of like-minded people there. In these enclaves, they could express their sexuality freely for the first time, and some of them took advantage of that freedom by having dozens or even hundreds of anonymous sexual encounters. The man in room 513 had followed this path.

By a seemingly strange coincidence, a physician acquaintance who treated gay men in Los Angeles phoned Gottlieb just a few weeks after Gottlieb saw the man in Room 516 and told him about three other young men who had *symptoms,* or signs of disease, similar to those that the UCLA patient had shown. These men, too, suffered from pneumocystis pneumonia and other *opportunistic infections,* illnesses caused by microbes that cannot harm healthy people but become dangerous to persons whose immune systems are too weak to repel them. Furthermore, the men's *lymph glands*—small organs under the arms, in the neck, and in several other parts of the body that hold collections of immune system cells—were swollen until they bulged under the skin like birds' eggs. This symptom also suggested a problem with the immune system.

Gottlieb heard about still another local patient with the same pattern of illness in early 1981. "The appearance . . . of . . . a fifth case suddenly made the thing look like a real epidemic," Dominique Lapierre's book about the start of the AIDS crisis, *Beyond Love,* quotes Gottlieb as saying. An epidemic is a major outbreak of infectious disease, or disease caused by microorganisms, in which many people suffer the same illness in about the same time and place.

REPORTS OF A NEW DISEASE

To warn other physicians about the seemingly new disease, Gottlieb wrote a short description of the five cases. The only scientific journal that would print it was a newsletter with the depressing name of *Morbidity and Mortality Weekly Report*. The *MMWR*, as people called it, was published by the Centers for Disease Control (CDC) in Atlanta, Georgia, the U.S. federal agency in charge of tracking and preventing infectious diseases. Gottlieb's article, "Pneumocystis Pneumonia—Los Angeles," appeared in the *MMWR* issue dated June 5, 1981. By this time, two of the five patients Gottlieb described had already died from their infections, and the others were near death.

The CDC, in fact, had indirect evidence of more cases like Gottlieb's. The agency controlled the supply of a drug called pentamidine, one of the few effective treatments for pneumocystis pneumonia, because the disease was so rare that the British pharmaceutical company that made the drug did not want to bother selling the medicine on its own. CDC records showed

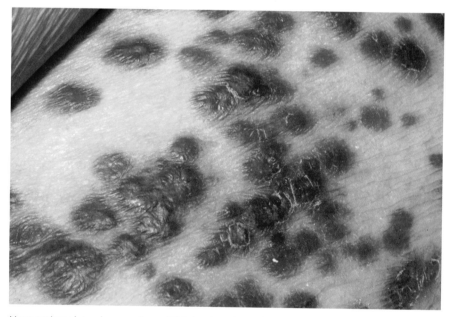

Many patients later shown to have AIDS developed purplish patches like these, the result of a formerly rare type of skin cancer called Kaposi's sarcoma. This cancer was shown in 1994 to be caused by a virus, human herpesvirus 8; it is one of many opportunistic infections that can strike people with AIDS. *(National Cancer Institute)*

that 16 physicians in different parts of the country had asked for pentamidine during just the first three months of 1981, whereas the agency had received only eight such requests during the entire previous year.

Meanwhile, in New York City, on the opposite side of the country from Michael Gottlieb, another physician was encountering an equally puzzling group of cases—also among young, previously healthy gay men. This physician, Alvin Friedman-Kien, was a dermatologist, or specialist in skin diseases, as well as a research scientist interested in viruses. He headed the department of dermatology and microbiology at the New York University Medical Center and was one of the first to use interferon, the substance Luc Montagnier had studied, as an antiviral drug.

In spring 1981, several doctors sent Friedman-Kien patients with purplish discolorations on their faces and bodies. Some of these men had swollen lymph glands as well. Friedman-Kien recognized the purple patches as signs of a rare form of skin cancer called *Kaposi's sarcoma*. He could hardly believe his own conclusion, however, because he knew that normally only elderly men who lived in or came from Africa, the Mediterranean area, or eastern Europe developed that disease. Furthermore, this type of cancer usually grew so slowly that its victims died of other causes before it did them much harm. A look at samples of the men's skin under a microscope told Friedman-Kien that his guess had been correct, but that only deepened his bewilderment. Why was this illness suddenly appearing in young white men and spreading rapidly through their bodies?

Just as Gottlieb had done with his cluster of pneumocystis pneumonia cases, Friedman-Kien began to wonder whether an unknown infectious disease lay behind the Kaposi outbreak. He asked other doctors who often treated homosexual patients whether they had seen anything like this condition, and he found that several had. So, he soon learned, had dermatologists with gay clients in San Francisco and nearby California cities.

Also like Gottlieb, Friedman-Kien wrote an article about his cases—which eventually numbered 26, including two who also had pneumocystis pneumonia—for the *MMWR*. It appeared in the July 3 issue, almost exactly a month after Gottlieb's report. The editor of the *MMWR* added a note after the article that connected the two reports, warning physicians to "be alert for Kaposi's sarcoma, pneumocystis pneumonia and other opportunistic infections associated with immunosuppression [reduced functioning of the immune system] in homosexual men."

THE FIRST AIDS CASES

Michael Gottlieb and Alvin Friedman-Kien were the first to report the disease later known as AIDS (acquired immune deficiency syndrome) in the medical literature. The patients they described, however, were certainly not the first to develop AIDS. Once alerted to the new *syndrome* (cluster of symptoms that usually occur together), physicians in the early 1980s searched their records and found a number of other cases that they or others had treated in the late 1970s without knowing what they were.

Later research uncovered occasional cases that had occurred even earlier. A black teenager in St. Louis, for instance, had died of opportunistic infections in 1969, and his doctors could find no reason why his immune system should have failed to control them. The physicians were so puzzled that they saved samples of his blood and tissue in the hope that later researchers might develop tests that could reveal what the young man had had. When the blood was tested in 1987, it showed signs of infection with the virus that by then had been shown to cause AIDS.

Another early probable AIDS victim was a Danish physician, Grethe Rask, who died of pneumocystis pneumonia in 1977. Rask had worked for several years as a surgeon in the Central African country then called Zaire. (Before gaining independence in 1960, it was the Belgian Congo; it is now known as the Democratic Republic of the Congo.) Like most doctors in Africa at the time, she had had to work with very limited medical equipment; for instance, she had to reuse syringes many times as she gave

CASES IN FRANCE

Only about 57,000 physicians subscribed to the *MMWR*, and few felt any interest in this strange group of illnesses that seemed to affect only people on the margins of society. One of those few was Willy Rozenbaum (1945–   ), a young doctor in Paris. Rozenbaum was a specialist in epidemiology, the study of the way diseases, especially infectious diseases, spread through groups of people. Michael Gottlieb's article caught his attention partly because later on the same day he read it he saw a patient who had exactly the same symptoms Gottlieb had described, as well as signs of a digestive ailment. The man, who was accompanied by a male friend, told Rozenbaum injections, and she often got patients' blood on her hands because she had no rubber gloves.

Like Grethe Rask, most of the other early AIDS cases (some verified through later testing of preserved blood samples, some guessed at from their symptoms) proved to have lived in or visited Central Africa. This gave researchers the first clue that the illness might have originated in that area. They suspected that it had occurred occasionally in the region for decades, perhaps longer. (Supporting this idea, the earliest verified AIDS case was later found to have occurred in 1959 in what is now the Democratic Republic of the Congo.) Only when a combination of social disruption, migration into crowded cities, and improved international travel increased people's movement in and out of the area, furthering contacts with strangers, did the disease begin to spread.

Researchers still are not sure how AIDS first reached North America, but many believe that the Caribbean island of Haiti was a likely stopover. A number of Haitians traveled to the Congo to work in the early 1960s, just after the area won its freedom from Belgium, and then returned home in the middle of the decade. Instances of the disease appeared in Haiti and in Haitian immigrants in Florida at about the same time that the first U.S. cases in non-Haitians were discovered. Genetic analysis suggested in 2007 that the most common strain of HIV, the virus that causes AIDS, probably traveled from Africa to Haiti around 1966 and moved on to the United States between 1969 and 1972.

that he was a steward for Air France. He thought he might have picked up an intestinal disease during a recent vacation in Egypt, but he also mentioned that he made frequent visits to New York and Los Angeles. Rozenbaum later told Dominique Lapierre:

It was as if something clicked in my head. The presence of the male companion at my patient's side and the mention of the frequent stopovers in Los Angeles made me link his illness to that of the young American homosexuals in the report I'd just been reading. I decided to try to get to the bottom of it at once.

Laboratory tests confirmed that Rozenbaum's patient had pneumocystis pneumonia, and Rozenbaum soon learned that a physician he knew, a specialist in chest diseases, had recently encountered several other men with this rare illness. Both doctors had the chilling thought that the underlying cause of the patients' immune system failure, whatever it might be, was spreading in Europe as well as in North America. The epidemic might well be worldwide.

Rozenbaum and two physician friends, Françoise Brun-Vézinet and Jacques Leibowitch, began to collect reports of similar symptoms. They tried to alert French medical researchers, including those at the Institut Pasteur, to the existence of this seemingly new disease, but at first their requests fell on deaf ears.

RISKY BEHAVIOR

Scientists at the National Institutes of Health (NIH) were equally uninterested when James Curran, the head of research on sexually transmitted diseases at the CDC, attempted to warn them about the possible epidemic in September 1981. Curran explained his belief that a single disease attacking the immune system lay behind the apparently separate outbreaks of pneumocystis pneumonia and Kaposi's sarcoma, but he failed to convince his hearers, primarily (he later told Dominique Lapierre) because "cancer experts had no experience with infectious diseases, and specialists in infectious diseases didn't have any with cancer." Robert Gallo was one of the NIH researchers who heard Curran's talk, but Gallo was deeply involved in his studies of HTLV and felt no desire to put that work aside and investigate what (he later told NIH historian Victoria Harden) appeared to be "an obscure disease [affecting] a small number of people."

The officials who allocated funding to NIH projects were also reluctant to become involved with what one (quoted in Dominique Lapierre's book) called "this pitiable little epidemic." Their attitude was not improved by the fact that by this time Curran and other CDC scientists had learned that the epidemic was spreading within a second group perhaps even more socially shunned than homosexuals: people who abused heroin and other *intravenous drugs* (those injected into the bloodstream). Most of the drug victims were not homosexual, but they shared needles with other drug users. These needles were seldom cleaned, which meant that they often carried traces of previous users' blood. The spread of the mystery disease among intravenous drug users suggested that blood could transmit the illness from one person to another.

The CDC itself was more supportive of Curran's efforts, granting him funding for a task force to investigate the possible epidemic. The task force focused on the first group to become sick: young gay men. After speaking informally with patients in Los Angeles, San Francisco, New York, and Miami, the CDC scientists designed a 500-item questionnaire, which they administered to about 50 men who showed signs of the new disease and 200 volunteers who followed a similar lifestyle but were healthy.

When Curran and his fellow scientists analyzed the men's answers in December, they found that the main difference between the sick and healthy groups was that the sick men had had 10 to 12 times as many sexual partners as the healthy ones. The CDC researchers were now fairly sure that the illness was caused by a microorganism, probably a virus, that was spread through sex, exchange of blood, and possibly in other ways. But was it a new virus or a familiar one acting in a new way because of an alteration in its genes? They conducted various tests on suspect viruses and eventually eliminated all of them.

Curran spoke again to scientists at the NIH, including Robert Gallo, in February 1982, but Gallo still doubted whether he wanted to search for the possible new virus. "The sensationalist aspect of [the epidemic], with all its disturbing and slightly distasteful implications, . . . put me resolutely off the venture," Gallo later told Dominique Lapierre. Gallo also feared for the safety of his staff. Of the 202 known people with the disease in the United States, 40 percent had died by this time, so it was obvious that whatever caused the illness was very dangerous. What if a laboratory worker became infected during the research and died? If such a tragedy occurred, Gallo wrote in his autobiography, he would have felt responsible.

THREAT TO THE BLOOD SUPPLY

In mid-1982, James Curran heard alarming news: A doctor in Denver, Colorado, had just requested pentamidine for a patient who belonged to neither of the known risk groups for the new disease. Instead, the man suffered from an inherited blood ailment called *hemophilia*. Hemophiliacs, as people with this illness are called, lack a substance that makes blood clot. They therefore can bleed to death from even a slight injury. Physicians had learned to treat this condition by extracting the missing compound, termed *Factor VIII*, from donated blood and giving it as a transfusion. Blood from thousands of people contributed to each transfusion of Factor VIII, and most hemophiliacs received many such transfusions during their lives.

The CDC learned of a second hemophiliac with the disease less than a week later. The fact that these people were developing the illness suggested a chilling probability: The disease agent not only could be spread through blood but had invaded the U.S. blood supply. Donated blood and blood products, such as Factor VIII, are filtered to remove bacteria and other relatively large microorganisms, but no filter can remove viruses. Thus, the new cases also added to the evidence that the disease agent was a virus.

The news soon became more disturbing still. In October 1982, a baby in San Francisco developed the symptoms of the mystery disease. Its parents were healthy, but the baby, sickly from birth, had been given numerous blood transfusions. Researchers in the city obtained the names of 13 people whose blood had been transfused into the baby, and they learned that one of these blood donors had died of the disease in August. There seemed to be no way the infant could have contracted the illness except through the transfusions.

Two months later, the *MMWR* reported on 22 more sick babies in New Jersey. These children had not received transfusions, but their mothers were either intravenous drug users or had come from the Caribbean island of Haiti, another place where cases of the strange illness were beginning to appear. It therefore seemed likely that they had caught the disease from their mothers. (Although most people reported to have the illness in the United States and Europe up to that time had been men, about equal numbers of men and women were affected in the Caribbean and Africa. Evidence was accumulating that the disease could be spread by sex between men and women as well as homosexual sex.)

In the early days of research on the new disease, some scientists had called it GRID, short for "gay-related immunodeficiency." By late 1982, however, it was obvious that this name was no longer appropriate. The CDC therefore decided to rename the illness AIDS, which stood for "acquired immune deficiency syndrome." The agency defined AIDS as a disease that strikes people under 60 years of age who have no other illness and are not undergoing any treatment that would depress their immune systems. It is marked by a severe shortage of CD4 lymphocytes and shows itself through the appearance of one or more opportunistic infections, especially pneumocystis pneumonia or Kaposi's sarcoma.

THE VIRUS HUNT BEGINS

Robert Gallo was now beginning to become interested in the mystery illness in spite of himself. Much of what had been learned about AIDS, after all,

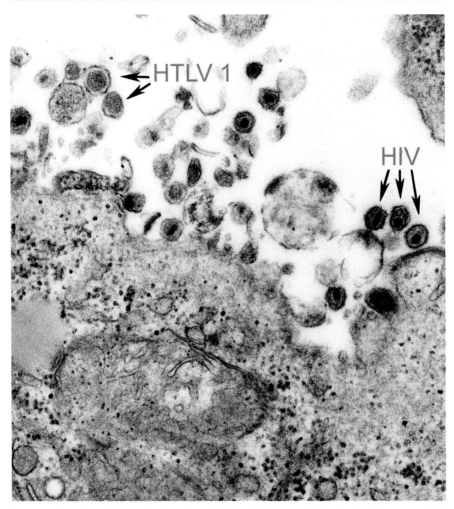

Some people with AIDS proved to be infected with both HTLV-1 and HIV, the virus that causes AIDS, so that both types of virus sometimes could be found in the same sample, as shown here. This helped to explain the confusion over whether HTLV-1 caused AIDS. *(Centers for Disease Control)*

sounded hauntingly familiar to him: It was probably caused by a virus, it seemed to spread through sex and blood, it specifically destroyed CD4 cells, and it had been found in sub-Saharan Africa and in the Caribbean. All these things were also true of HTLV-1, the cancer-causing virus that Gallo had so recently discovered. He could hardly help wondering whether HTLV-1 or a closely related retrovirus might cause the new disease as well.

Gallo finally decided to become involved after Jacques Leibowitch, one of the young Parisian doctors studying AIDS, visited him in July 1982.

Leibowitch brought Gallo blood samples from all the French victims of the new disease that he could find, including three who had lived for a long time in Africa and another who had received a blood transfusion while in Haiti. Given this wealth of promising material, Gallo could no longer resist. That fall he assigned Prem Sarin, a researcher from India who worked in his laboratory, to begin hunting for the mystery virus by trying to find reverse transcriptase in Leibowitch's samples. By the end of the year, they had identified the enzyme in some samples, but electron micrographs had not revealed the virus that produced it.

French researchers—including Luc Montagnier—were also beginning to realize that the new epidemic was too important to ignore. Montagnier, who had missed hearing Willy Rozenbaum's speech to the Pasteur scientists in late 1981, first learned about AIDS when Paul Prunet, science director of the Institut Pasteur Production (IPP), paid him a visit in November 1982. The IPP, the institute's commercial arm, manufactured vaccines and medical tests developed from Pasteur scientists' discoveries. One of these vaccines, which protected people against the hepatitis B virus (the cause of a severe liver disease), used blood products imported from the United States. Prunet had heard reports of a new illness possibly being spread through blood in that country, and he wanted Montagnier to help him find out whether the IPP vaccine was safe. Shortly afterward, Françoise Brun-Vézinet, who had once been a student of Montagnier's at the institute, phoned Montagnier with the story of what she, Rozenbaum, and Leibowitch had learned. She, too, urged him to begin looking for the cause of AIDS.

Like Robert Gallo, Montagnier suspected that the AIDS agent was a retrovirus, possibly related to HTLV. In late December, he asked Jean-Claude Chermann and Françoise Sinoussi to begin testing samples of the imported blood products for reverse transcriptase activity. The hunt was on.

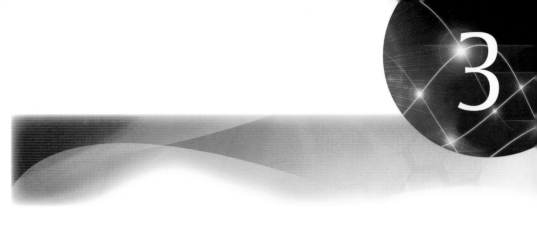

Search for the Virus

At first, the virus hunters at the Institut Pasteur had no luck: Luc Montagnier, Jean-Claude Chermann, and Françoise Barré-Sinoussi could find no reverse transcriptase in either blood products or the cells of AIDS victims. Soon, however, Willy Rozenbaum began to suspect they were choosing the wrong targets. He knew that by the time a patient showed clear signs of AIDS, most of the person's T cells had already vanished. He thought that the Pasteur scientists might have a better chance of finding the mystery virus or its reverse transcriptase "footprint" if they looked at the blood or lymph gland tissue of people who had just begun to be sick, which might still contain quite a few virus-filled cells. Examining material from people in the early stages of the disease, before opportunistic infections invaded their bodies, would also reduce the chances that any virus in the sample was simply a random invader. Rozenbaum said he would send them such material.

On January 3, 1983, Françoise Brun-Vézinet, Montagnier's former student, brought the French group the tissue that Rozenbaum had promised. In a little test tube buried in a container of dry ice she carried a fresh *biopsy* sample (a small piece of tissue removed for doctors to examine in order to diagnose disease) of a lymph gland taken from Frédéric Brugière, a gay fashion designer who was a patient of Rozenbaum's. Brugière had persistent swollen lymph glands, often an early sign of AIDS, but he had not yet developed the full-blown disease.

Jean-Claude Chermann (*left*), Françoise Barré-Sinoussi, and Luc Montagnier worked together to isolate the virus later shown to cause AIDS. They are shown here in Chermann's laboratory at the Institut Pasteur in the mid-1980s. (*Institut Pasteur*)

Montagnier was teaching a class when Brun-Vézinet arrived, but he found the tube in his refrigerator when he came back to the laboratory around dinnertime. He extracted cells from the lymph gland tissue and put them in another tube with substances that he hoped would encourage them to multiply, including both his own anti-interferon serum and Robert Gallo's interleukin-2. He labeled the culture Bru, from the first three letters of Brugière's last name.

FIRST SIGNS OF A VIRUS

To minimize the risk of contaminating their cultures with animal viruses, Montagnier and his coworkers wanted to carry out their AIDS research in a space that was separate from the rest of their laboratory and other experiments. They chose a little room next to Chermann's laboratory, a former laundry room, and named it "the Bru room" in Brugière's honor.

Every three days, Françoise Barré-Sinoussi went to the Bru room to test cells in the growing culture for reverse transcriptase, using a marker chemical that would produce radioactivity if the enzyme was present. Her counters showed only background radiation at first. She obtained her first positive reading in mid-January, but the radioactivity level was still so low that it might have been a mistake. Then, however, the radiation count began climbing.

Montagnier's team was thrilled with their progress—but triumph soon turned to dismay. By late January, the T cells in the precious Bru culture were starting to die, as cells usually do after a short period in culture. "We were finding the virus at the same time we were losing it," Jean-Claude Chermann later told *Chicago Tribune* reporter John Crewdson, as Crewdson recounts in *Science Fictions*. Since the group could find nothing else in their cultures that might harm the cells, they concluded that the unknown virus must be killing them. This was just the opposite of what they would expect if the virus was Gallo's HTLV-1. As a cancer-causing virus, HTLV-1 made cells multiply indefinitely.

The group could find no way to rescue their culture until Montagnier thought to feed the ravenous virus with new, healthy T cells. He obtained these cells first from adult blood donors and then, following a suggestion from another team member, from the blood of newborn babies that was trapped in their umbilical cords, the rope of blood vessels that connects a baby in the womb to its mother's blood supply. Doctors normally cut off the umbilical cord and discard it after a child's birth, but researchers sometimes use blood from umbilical cords in experiments. The Bru culture grew even more vigorously with these infant cells than it had with the adult ones. When Montagnier examined the cells under a microscope, however, he saw no sign that the cells had become cancerous.

Excitedly, the group sent a sample of their cells to Charles Dauguet, Pasteur's electron microscopist. Dauguet scanned and photographed them, hoping to catch virus particles in the act of breaking free from the cells. On February 4, he finally spotted some. They were pear-shaped, with a black core shaped like a cone or a bar. Dauguet's first pictures were blurry, but later in the month he took better ones. The viruses in his photographs did not look anything like the ones in photos that Gallo's research team had taken of HTLV, which had round or disclike cores.

Montagnier's team also used a centrifuge, a device that spins test tubes of biological material at a very high rate of speed, to separate a sample from their culture into cells and a liquid that was expected to contain the virus. They put the cell-free liquid into a new culture of healthy T cells and showed that it made the cells start to die. That effect provided powerful, though still indirect, evidence that the original culture really did contain a virus.

FRANÇOISE BARRÉ-SINOUSSI (1947–   ): CODISCOVERER OF THE AIDS VIRUS

Françoise Sinoussi was born in Paris on July 30, 1947. Her childhood pets, a cat, a mouse, and a parakeet, provided her with "the observations that . . . inspired . . . enthusiasm for the treasures contained in the great book of life," she told Dominique Lapierre. A friend introduced her to Jean-Claude Chermann while she was working on her master's degree in biochemistry (which she obtained in 1972) at the Sciences Faculty at the University of Paris. Chermann became her mentor and brought her to the Institut Pasteur, where she obtained her Ph.D. in virology in 1975. She did postdoctoral work on retroviruses at the U.S. National Cancer Institute (NCI) in 1975–76 at a laboratory near Robert Gallo's and met some of the researchers in his group at that time.

When Sinoussi returned to France, she rejoined the Institut Pasteur under the sponsorship of INSERM, the French National Institute for Health and Medical Research. She was a research assistant until 1980, an assistant professor from 1980 to 1986, and a research director thereafter. She married, changing her name to Barré-Sinoussi, around 1982. The Institut Pasteur gave her her own retrovirus biology laboratory in 1986, and she became head of the retrovirus biology unit (now called the regulation of retroviral infections unit) in 1992. In 1996, she was made a full professor. She was deputy director to the scientific affairs of the international network of the Institut Pasteur from 2001 to 2005.

Barré-Sinoussi has focused on AIDS since 1983, when her meticulous work with cell cultures in Luc Montagnier's laboratory led to the discovery of the virus later known as HIV. Her research specialty has been mother-to-child transmission of the virus and the attempts of the immune system to control the infection. She has played major roles in several international AIDS organizations, including the Joint United Nations Programme on HIV/AIDS (UNAIDS) and the French National Agency on AIDS Research (ANRS). She shared the 2008 Nobel Prize in physiology or medicine with Luc Montagnier for her part in the discovery of HIV and has won many other awards as well. She is an officer of the French Legion of Honor (2006) and a member of the Women in Technology International Hall of Fame (2007).

COMPETING VIRUSES

But what virus had the French researchers discovered? For a start, Montagnier's group knew they had to find out whether their virus could be HTLV—or verify their suspicion that it was not. They asked Robert Gallo therefore to send them serum containing antibodies to HTLV, and he did so in late February.

Each kind of antibody that the immune system makes is different, built to attach itself to the single type of "foreign" molecule (part of the coat of a bacterium or virus, for instance) that triggers its formation. Antibodies to HTLV, therefore, would cling only to cells containing that particular virus. Montagnier's group mixed a sample of their Bru culture with the serum Gallo had sent, then washed the sample. If the sample contained HTLV, they expected antibodies from the serum to remain on some of the cells. They could detect these antibodies by means of marker chemicals attached to them. If the Bru virus was not HTLV, on the other hand, the antibodies would be washed away, and the team would see no sign of the markers.

Montagnier's team found that antibodies to HTLV did not cling to the Bru cells, providing further evidence that the virus in the cells was not HTLV. Françoise Barré-Sinoussi later told Dominique Lapierre that they were so thrilled at what they saw under their microscope that "we could have danced in a circle around it." The group also found that antibodies in Brugière's own blood attached to the virus in the cell culture, which provided further evidence that the virus in the culture was not a contaminant.

Robert Gallo was now devoting more of his laboratory's time to the search for a virus that might cause AIDS. The disease had begun to attract widespread media attention at the end of 1982, after reporters learned that babies and blood transfusion recipients were developing it, and Vincent DeVita, then director of the NCI, formed a task force to find the virus in April 1983 and placed Gallo in charge of it. Prem Sarin, the lone researcher whom Gallo had originally assigned to the AIDS research, had had little success, so Gallo put additional laboratory members on the project.

The Gallo group examined numerous blood and tissue samples, including some that Jacques Leibowitch had brought from Paris in February. They were excited to see that cell cultures from two of Leibowitch's samples, one taken from a Haitian woman and the other from a French geologist who had received a blood transfusion while visiting Haiti, appeared to contain retroviruses. Like Montagnier's team, however, they found that the cells in their cultures kept dying, no matter how carefully the researchers tended them.

In spite of this behavior, Gallo was sure that the viruses would prove to be HTLV-1 or a close relative. To be sure, AIDS seemed to be the exact opposite of leukemia: People with leukemia had too many white cells, whereas people with AIDS had almost none. Nonetheless, Gallo knew of a single virus that could produce such contradictory effects. Myron (Max) Essex, a scientist at the Harvard University School of Public Health in Boston, had told him about *feline leukemia virus (FeLV),* which, as its name indicates, sometimes causes a fatal blood cell cancer in cats. At least equally often, however, the virus destroys cells in the cats' immune systems, leaving the animals vulnerable to opportunistic infections—just like AIDS patients. Gallo thought that HTLV might be able to affect humans in the same way that FeLV affects cats.

PAPERS IN *SCIENCE*

By April 1983, Luc Montagnier felt sure enough of having found a new human retrovirus that he wanted to publish an account of his laboratory's work. Such a virus, after all, would be a major discovery, whether or not the virus proved to be the cause of AIDS. He had planned to submit his paper to *Nature,* a prestigious journal that focuses on research in Europe, but Gallo recommended that he instead send the paper to *Science, Nature*'s equivalent in the United States. Gallo said that his laboratory was planning to submit several papers about their own AIDS research to the magazine, and he thought it would make sense for Montagnier's paper to appear in the same issue. Montagnier agreed to do so.

The submission deadline for the *Science* issue that Gallo had mentioned was coming soon, so Montagnier hurriedly finished a draft of his paper. When a paper is submitted to a science journal, the editors normally send copies of the article to several of the author's peers—other scientists of approximately equal rank, working in the same field—and ask for their comments on it before deciding whether to publish it. Montagnier knew that anything he wrote about human retroviruses was bound to go to Gallo, so he sent the paper directly to the NCI scientist rather than to the magazine in order to save time.

In his rush to complete his paper, Montagnier forgot to write the abstract, a brief summary of the paper's contents that normally appears just before the article itself. Gallo noticed this missing part and offered to write the abstract himself before sending the paper on to *Science* with his review. Without thinking much about it, Montagnier agreed. Gallo read his abstract to Montagnier and Barré-Sinoussi over the telephone, but Barré-Sinoussi later told John Crewdson that the French scientists had had trouble taking in the exact wording of what he said.

The May 20 issue of *Science* contained two papers from Gallo's laboratory and two from Max Essex as well as the paper that Montagnier and his coworkers had written. The title of the news article in the same issue that summarized these five featured papers underlined the main point of the research findings—at least as Robert Gallo saw it: "Human T-Cell Leukemia Virus Linked to AIDS." By that time, according to the article's author, Jean L. Marx, more than 1,350 cases of AIDS had been reported to the CDC, and the illness was fatal to more than 70 percent of its victims. Marx listed Gallo's reasons for believing that HTLV-1 might cause AIDS: Both AIDS and HTLV-1 were common in the Caribbean and Africa, both affected T cells, and both appeared to be transmitted in similar ways. She also mentioned FeLV as an example of a virus that could cause either leukemia or immune system suppression, as HTLV-1 would have to be able to do if it caused AIDS. (One of Essex's papers reported that natural infection by FeLV often crippled cats' immune systems.)

Marx stressed that it was too soon to say that HTLV-1 was the cause of AIDS rather than simply an opportunistic infection. However, she said, the five papers provided good evidence for believing that the virus was at least associated with the disease. One of the Gallo laboratory's papers reported finding a copy of the HTLV-1 genome—a provirus, in other words—in the DNA of T cells from two of 33 AIDS patients (the two Haitian samples that had come from Leibowitch), but not in the cells of any of 25 healthy homosexual men. Cells from another culture, Gallo said in a second paper, had yielded virus particles that could be identified as HTLV-1, both from their appearance and from the fact that antibodies to HTLV-1 reacted with them. Marx also described Essex's report that 25 to 30 percent of AIDS patients, but not healthy homosexual men, had antibodies to a cell membrane protein found only on cells infected with HTLV-1, good if indirect evidence that the patients were or had been infected with the virus. She devoted only a sentence to the Montagnier group's paper, saying merely that the Pasteur laboratory had "isolated a related virus"—that is, a virus related to HTLV-1—from a single patient with swollen lymph glands.

When Montagnier saw the magazine, he was dismayed to discover that Gallo had written the abstract for his paper in a way that stressed the similarities between the French virus and HTLV-1 and even exaggerated some of them, whereas the paper itself emphasized similarities and differences about equally. The abstract therefore made Montagnier's appear to be simply a confirmation of Gallo's claims about HTLV-1, rather than the striking new finding that it was. Montagnier later told John Crewdson that he thought Gallo had been so convinced that the French virus must be closely related to HTLV-1 that he had seen what he wanted to see in Montagnier's paper and therefore had misunderstood its meaning.

CLASSIFYING THE VIRUS

Although Montagnier's group believed that they had discovered a new human retrovirus that might well be the cause of AIDS, they knew that they had by no means proved this. To begin with, they would have to find the same virus, or antibodies to it, in a variety of blood and tissue samples from people with AIDS, preferably people that belonged to all the different risk groups then known: homosexual men, intravenous drug abusers, hemophiliacs, people who had received blood transfusions, Haitians, Africans, and women partners of men with the disease. The Pasteur team would also have to show that healthy people did not have the virus or antibodies that reacted with it. They examined numerous samples during the spring and summer of 1983 and isolated what appeared to be the same virus from two of them. Cells from one of these samples, taken from a French student named Christophe Lailier and labeled Lai, grew and produced viruses even more vigorously than those from the group's first culture, Bru.

The Montagnier team chose a name for their virus in June 1983. They called all the viruses taken from people with swollen lymph glands *LAV*, which stood for lymphadenopathy-associated virus. (*Lymphadenopathy* is the medical term for swollen lymph glands. At that time, this condition was considered to be either a forerunner of AIDS or a mild form of the disease.) They referred to the ones isolated from people with full-blown AIDS as IDAV (immune-deficiency-associated virus). They felt sure, however, that all the viruses were really the same. They continued to identify particular cell cultures (and the viruses that grew in them) with the first three letters of the names of the patients from whom the cells had first come. Frédéric Brugière's culture and virus strain, for instance, was LAV-Bru.

Around this time, David Klatzmann, an immunologist (scientist who studies the immune system) in Willy Rozenbaum's group, showed that LAV grew only in CD4 lymphocytes, the exact type of cells known to be depleted in people with AIDS, and killed the infected cells. Montagnier later told John

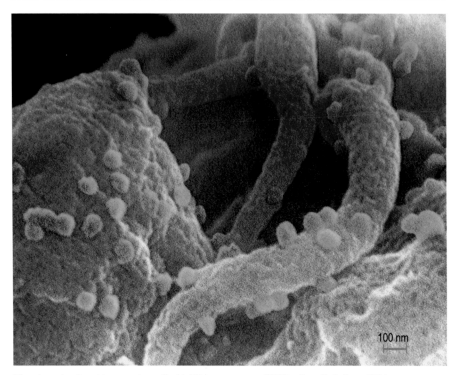

The virus that Luc Montagnier called LAV, later renamed HIV, primarily infects CD4 lymphocytes. This scanning electron micrograph shows the virus, in green, growing among lymphocytes. *(CDC/C. Goldsmith, P. Feorino, E. L. Palmer, W. R. McManus)*

Crewdson that this work was "one of the critical proofs that the virus [LAV] was the cause of AIDS."

Meanwhile, Françoise Brun-Vézinet and Christine Rouzioux, both of whom joined the Montagnier laboratory that summer, began preparing a test that would let them identify antibodies to LAV in samples of blood. It would be a form of blood test called *ELISA,* or *enzyme-linked immunosorbent assay.* ELISA tests were already used to spot infection with certain other viruses, such as the ones that cause hepatitis. Such tests not only helped doctors determine the cause of patients' illnesses but screened donated blood so that blood contaminated by dangerous microorganisms could be rejected.

Montagnier, for his part, became more convinced than ever that LAV was not closely related to HTLV-1 when he showed Charles Dauguet's photographs of the virus to another Institut Pasteur virologist Oswald Edlinger. Edlinger told Montagnier that the virus looked very much like the infectious equine anemia virus, which causes a blood disease in horses. This virus belongs to a group that is called the *lentiviruses,* or slow viruses, because the illnesses they cause appear several years after infection. This retrovirus family is quite different from the one that includes HTLV-1. Montagnier found that antibodies to a core protein in the horse virus—the protein that varies the least among members of a retrovirus family—reacted to the core protein of LAV, which provided further evidence that the two viruses were related. However, LAV would not grow in horse lymphocytes, nor would the horse virus grow in human ones. The horse virus also did not attack CD4 lymphocytes or produce immune suppression in the animals it infected. Montagnier concluded, therefore, that the two viruses were at most "very distant cousins," as he wrote in *Virus.* Still, he believed that LAV was far more closely related to this and other lentiviruses than to Gallo's HTLVs.

DISAPPOINTING RECEPTION

Robert Gallo invited Luc Montagnier to speak at the first meeting of the National Cancer Institute's task force on AIDS, held in Bethesda, Maryland, in July 1983. He also asked for a sample of LAV to compare with the viruses growing in his own laboratory. Montagnier agreed to attend and bring the virus with him. Before he did so, however, the Institut Pasteur's patent coordinator, Danielle Berneman, deposited a sample of LAV in France's National Collection of Microorganism Cultures. This step was required before technology related to the virus, such as the Montagnier group's blood test, could be patented. If LAV did prove to be the cause of AIDS, the blood test for it was likely to be widely used, and a patent on it might become very valuable.

Montagnier arrived in the United States on July 17 with three tubes of virus packed in dry ice. He took the sample container to Gallo's home, where a volleyball game was going on. He was startled to see Gallo casually place the container in his freezer and go back to his guests.

The next morning, Montagnier described his work with LAV to the scientists in the NCI task force, which included representatives from the CDC and several university laboratories working on AIDS. Few, however, seemed to be listening; Montagnier complained in his autobiography that the meeting was "a festival for HTLV." Almost no one appeared to grasp his claim that LAV was very different from HTLV-1—except perhaps NCI electron microscopist Matthew Gonda, who agreed that LAV looked far more like a lentivirus than like a relative of Gallo's virus. Montagnier had originally planned to continue his collaboration with Gallo, but now, as he wrote in

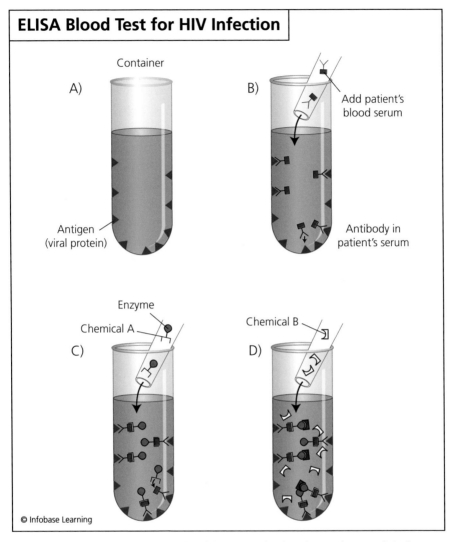

ELISA Blood Test for HIV Infection

Container

A)

Antigen
(viral protein)

B)

Add patient's
blood serum

Antibody in
patient's serum

Enzyme

Chemical A

C)

Chemical B

D)

© Infobase Learning

Both Luc Montagnier's and Robert Gallo's laboratories developed ELISA (enzyme-linked immunosorbent assay) tests to identify antibodies to the AIDS virus in a sample of blood, a sign that the virus has infected the sample's donor. Other ELISA tests reveal antibodies to surface proteins (antigens) from other microorganisms. An ELISA test kit contains a test tube with virus proteins or other antigens attached to the sides (A). If blood containing antibodies that fit those proteins is added to the tube, the antibodies stick to the antigens and cannot be washed away (B). An enzyme attached to a marker chemical (chemical A) is then added, and it, in turn, attaches to the antibodies (C). After a second washing, another chemical (chemical B) is added. This chemical glows or changes color when it reacts with chemical A, which will happen only if chemical A has attached to the antibodies and therefore is still present (D). The glow or color change counts as a positive result, showing that antibodies to the antigen—and therefore the source of the antigen itself, in this case the AIDS virus—can be found in the sample.

Virus, "overcome with exasperation that no attention had really been paid to our new virus," he withdrew the offer.

The Montagnier team completed their ELISA test for LAV by the end of the summer. They showed that more than 60 percent of patients with lymphadenopathy had antibodies to the virus, which strongly suggested that the people were infected with it. Only about a fifth of people with full-blown AIDS showed the antibodies, however. Rouzioux and Brun-Vézinet were not sure whether this meant that LAV caused lymphadenopathy but not AIDS or whether people with AIDS simply had too little immune system left to form antibodies. The Institut Pasteur applied for a European patent on the test in early September.

In August, while his two laboratory mates were finishing their work on the blood test, Montagnier sent letters to several French national research agencies, warning them that the virus he had discovered was "potentially dangerous" and might be present in banked blood and blood products. He asked for help in commercializing and distributing the Pasteur ELISA test so that donated blood in France could be screened. He also requested more funding and facilities for his own laboratory, including a room that would be equipped to handle deadly viruses safely.

Neither the agencies nor the directors of his own institute showed much interest, however. They pointed out that only about 100 cases of AIDS had appeared in France. Furthermore, they said, Montagnier's research might well be wrong; after all, it contradicted the ideas of that world-renowned expert on retroviruses, Robert Gallo.

Painful Rivalry

Perhaps this time Luc Montagnier would finally be able to make U.S. scientists listen to his ideas. He would have a chance to present them on September 14 and 15, 1983, at a scientific meeting about human retroviruses that was expected to attract the most eminent specialists in the country. The meeting would be held at Cold Spring Harbor Laboratories, a famous molecular biology research center on Long Island, New York. Montagnier knew that being allowed to read a paper at a Cold Spring Harbor meeting was a high honor.

Montagnier's opportunity was not as great as it might have seemed, however. Like the meeting of the National Cancer Institute task force in July, the Cold Spring Harbor gathering proved to be a "festival for HTLV." Robert Gallo and Max Essex, the organizers of the conference, assigned only one session of it to AIDS, and they placed that session at the very end, when many of the attendees had already left.

HARSH CRITICISM

Luc Montagnier had only 20 minutes to speak during the AIDS session at the Cold Spring Harbor conference. Into that short time, he tried to pack an account of all his laboratory had discovered during the past nine very busy months: descriptions and photos of the viruses the group had isolated from five patients with AIDS or pre-AIDS, LAV's similarities to the equine infectious anemia virus, the fact that LAV specifically attacked CD4 cells, and the team's new ELISA test.

Gallo himself attended the session. During the question period that followed Montagnier's talk, the Bethesda scientist fired a stream of critical questions at his French colleague. Montagnier wrote in his autobiography that when he asked Gallo afterward why he had been so hostile, Gallo said, "You punched me out"—meaning that Montagnier had essentially disproved his claims that the cause of AIDS would prove to be HTLV or a similar virus. Speaking of Montagnier, Gallo wrote in his own autobiography, *Virus Hunting:*

> We are not alike in our styles, as people or as scientists. He is quiet, almost formal, holding his own counsel [that is, keeping silent] when competing ideas are being presented [whereas] . . . I love the rough-and-tumble of intellectual debate.

Nonetheless, Gallo wrote, he was later sorry that he had spoken so sharply.

> I have often thought about how much simpler [my] life might have been over the next few years had I not led the charge that day. . . . I have come increasingly to regret that the tone or spirit of my questioning . . . was too aggressive and therefore misunderstood.

The other scientists at the session were not as outspoken as Gallo, but most of them also did not seem convinced that Montagnier was correct. Montagnier wrote that he felt he was up against "a wall of indifference and bad faith." Even in 1994, when he wrote *Virus,* Montagnier said that he and his laboratory mates still had "a feeling of bitterness about this period. We knew we were right, but we were the only ones."

PERMANENT VIRUS CULTURES

In spite of their clash at the Cold Spring Harbor meeting, Gallo asked Montagnier for still more samples of LAV, claiming that his laboratory had not been able to grow the July samples in cell cultures. Montagnier agreed, but he insisted that someone from the laboratory first sign a document promising that any material he sent would be used only for research, not for commercial purposes such as developing a blood test. When the document arrived at Bethesda a little later, Gallo was out of the country at a scientific conference, so Mikulas (Mika) Popovic, one of Gallo's chief researchers, signed it. On receiving the signed copy, Montagnier prepared the requested samples, and Françoise Barré-Sinoussi took them to Bethesda in late September.

By this time, evidence was beginning to accumulate that Montagnier rather than Gallo was right about the AIDS virus. In October, Popovic tested cells from AIDS patients with serums containing antibodies to HTLV-1 and to LAV. About 10 percent of the samples reacted with both serums, suggesting that the people who had donated them were infected with both viruses. All, however, reacted to the anti-LAV serum, providing strong evidence that Montagnier's virus was present. "At that moment, I came to the conclusion that we were wrong [in thinking that HTLV-1 causes AIDS] and Barré-Sinoussi was right," Popovic told a NIH inquiry board, the Office of Scientific Integrity, in 1990. Even Gallo no longer insisted (at least in private) that the AIDS virus would prove to be HTLV-1, but he still thought that it would be a related virus. "The overall evidence [at this time] suggested to me that this was a new human retrovirus, one likely related to the HTLVs," he wrote in *Virus Hunting.*

In addition to LAV, Gallo's laboratory had some cell cultures of their own that they believed to contain the AIDS virus. They, too, hoped to develop an ELISA test that would identify antibodies to the virus in patients' or donors' blood. Both laboratories knew that in order to carry out more experiments on their viruses, let alone provide the supply of virus that companies manufacturing the blood tests would need (since the test kits would have to contain proteins from the target virus), they had to find a way to grow large amounts of their virus dependably. This was a particular challenge for viruses that might cause AIDS, since the candidate viruses regularly killed the cells they infected.

The best way to produce an assured source of virus would be to persuade the virus to grow in a *cell line,* a group of cells that had been converted to a cancerlike state so they would multiply indefinitely in a laboratory culture. Researchers in many laboratories had developed lines from different kinds of cells and made cultures of them available to other scientists on request.

Both the Montagnier and the Gallo groups succeeded in transferring their viruses to cell lines in the fall of 1983. The French team could not make LAV grow in any line of T cells, but they successfully transferred it to a line of B cells, another type of immune system cell. Mika Popovic, the scientist in charge of this task in Gallo's laboratory, at first had little luck with T cell lines either, but he finally succeeded by taking the unusual step of pooling, or combining, material from several different AIDS patients. Virologists normally do not do this because if a virus from such a pool does begin to infect cells, there is no way to determine which patient the virus came from—information that can be important in understanding the virus and, if necessary, obtaining more samples of it. Popovic knew, however, that different strains of the same virus can grow with different degrees of vigor, as Montagnier had found out with Bru and Lai. He hoped that pooling the samples would speed up the process of finding a virus strain strong enough to infect a cell line and that this advantage would outweigh the drawback of not knowing the exact source of the virus.

Popovic's hunch proved to be correct. In November, shortly after Montagnier's team had succeeded with their B cell line, a virus from Popovic's pool began growing in a T cell line in Gallo's laboratory. Popovic at once began using it to develop an ELISA test of his own.

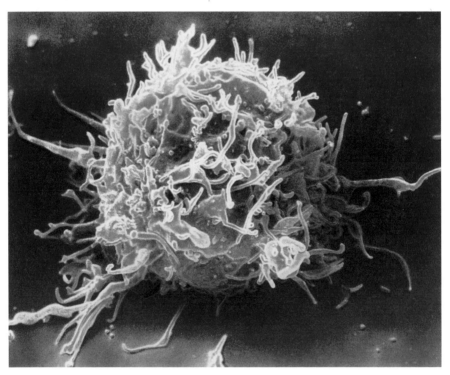

The AIDS virus kills normal T cells, like those shown here. Keeping the virus growing in a laboratory culture therefore was difficult. Both Montagnier's and Gallo's laboratories eventually succeeded in producing continuous cultures of the virus, however. *(NIBSC/Photo Researchers, Inc.)*

MATHILDE KRIM (1926–   ) AND AMFAR: SUPPORTING AIDS RESEARCH

In the early days of the AIDS epidemic, funding for research on the disease was extremely limited in both France and the United States. The first person to establish a private organization to support AIDS research was Mathilde Galland Krim, who set up the AIDS Medical Foundation in New York in April 1983.

Krim herself was a scientist. Born in Italy but raised in Switzerland, she had helped to develop amniocentesis, a technique for obtaining genetic information about an unborn child by sampling the fluid that surrounds the fetus in the uterus, in the 1950s. In 1958, she married Arthur B. Krim, a wealthy U.S. lawyer and film executive, and moved to New York. She studied viruses, especially cancer-causing retroviruses, first at Cornell Medical College and then at the renowned Sloan-Kettering Institute for Cancer Research. In the late 1970s, her research, like Luc Montagnier's, focused on interferon.

In 1981, a physician friend of Krim's, Joseph Sonnabend (1932–   ), told her about seeing pneumocystis pneumonia and Kaposi's sarcoma in his gay patients. As word about the growing AIDS epidemic began to spread, Krim became concerned about the lack of support for research on the disease. She decided to use her and her husband's contacts in Hollywood, New York society, and the world of politics to increase understanding of AIDS and raise money for research on it. According to Jonathan Engel's The Epidemic: A Global History of AIDS, "Krim quickly became one of the most visible advocates for AIDS research outside of the gay community, and managed nearly single-handedly to legitimize the disease as a charity for more establishment-minded philanthropists."

Krim's AIDS Medical Foundation merged with the National AIDS Research Foundation, a similar organization founded by Michael Gottlieb, the Los Angeles doctor who had written the first medical paper on AIDS, in September 1985. Krim and Gottlieb became cochairs of the new organization, which they called the American Foundation for AIDS Research (amfAR). The group attracted the support of some of the country's most

(continues)

(continued)

famous movie stars, including Rock Hudson (1925–85), who gave the new organization $250,000 just before dying of AIDS in October 1985, and Elizabeth Taylor (1932–2011), who was very active in AIDS charity work almost from the beginning of the epidemic. In addition to funding research, amfAR tried to educate legislators and the public about the disease in the hope of reducing the fear and rejection that people with AIDS often faced.

AmfAR has kept its initials, but in 2005 it changed its name to the Foundation for AIDS Research to reflect its present international focus. According to the organization's Web site, amfAR has provided nearly $290 million to more than 2,000 research groups worldwide since its inception.

Many people with AIDS and their supporters felt during the early years of the epidemic that government and established charities were ignoring the disease because most of its victims belonged to groups that society did not respect. Some formed activist groups and protested, like these people carrying a banner up Market Street in San Francisco during the 13th annual Gay Freedom Day parade in 1983. Others, like Mathilde Krim, tried more quiet means of educating people about the disease and raising money for AIDS research. (AP Images)

"THESE GUYS HAVE SOMETHING"

By the end of 1983, several research groups besides Montagnier's and Gallo's, including one at the Centers for Disease Control and Prevention (CDC) and one led by Jay Levy at the University of California, San Francisco, were also studying viruses they had isolated from AIDS patients, working on blood tests, or both. Levy had found a virus that he believed to be the cause of AIDS in November 1983, and the CDC located their virus in December. The link between the CDC team's virus and AIDS was especially convincing because the team's virus samples had come from a matched pair of people: a woman who had acquired AIDS from a blood transfusion and the donor who had provided the blood. No one yet knew for sure whether any of these viruses were identical to one another or to Montagnier's LAV, although the CDC, to whom Montagnier had given samples of LAV, believed that their virus was the same.

A second important scientific meeting about possible AIDS viruses took place in Park City, Utah, in February 1984. This time Jean-Claude Chermann represented the French team. Chermann had better success in interesting other scientists in LAV than Montagnier had had at Cold Spring Harbor. According to John Crewdson's *Science Fictions,* Michael Gottlieb, one of the organizers of the meeting, recalled, "People were sitting there ready to go skiing and all of a sudden there were people saying, 'Hey, these guys have something.'"

Montagnier's and Gallo's laboratories continued to improve the ELISA tests for their respective viruses in early 1984. Both obtained excellent results with a large number of samples that the CDC supplied. Almost all the blood samples from AIDS patients tested positive—that is, antibodies in the blood attached themselves to the virus proteins in the test kits—but blood samples from healthy people showed no reaction (tested negative). This matching was particularly convincing because of an important difference between retroviruses and other viruses or microorganisms. As Robert Gallo pointed out in his autobiography, finding antibodies to a certain microorganism in a person's blood often means only that the microbe has entered that person's body at some time in the past; it may not even have caused disease, or if it did, the illness may have ended long ago. With retroviruses, however, antibodies to the virus are present only if infection with that virus is still going on. The fact that the two laboratories' test results matched one another as well as matching the diagnoses convinced James Curran that both laboratories really had found the cause of AIDS.

Gallo told Montagnier in March 1984 that he was positive that his, Gallo's, laboratory had isolated the virus that causes AIDS. He called the virus *HTLV-3*. Gallo later wrote in his autobiography that he intended this name to mean only that the virus was a new human retrovirus that attacked T cells; according to him, a group of scientists at the September 1983 Cold Spring Harbor meeting had agreed to name all human retroviruses infecting T lymphocytes in order of their discovery, whether they were related to one another or not and whether they caused leukemia or not. To Montagnier, however, the name suggested that Gallo was still claiming a relationship between the virus and his earlier finds, HTLV-1 and HTLV-2—a relationship that Montagnier felt sure did not exist.

ONE-SIDED ANNOUNCEMENT

Robert Gallo was planning to publish several papers about his virus in the May 4 issue of *Science*. This magazine, like many other science journals, had a policy that prohibited researchers publishing in their pages from announcing their discoveries to the media before their articles were printed. Nonetheless, several stories appeared in British and U.S. newspapers in April, claiming that Gallo's laboratory, Montagnier's, or both, would soon announce that they had found the long-sought cause of AIDS. Because of these leaks, Margaret Heckler (1931–   ), secretary of health and human services (HHS), the government department that oversees the National Institutes of Health (NIH), felt that she needed to make a public statement about Gallo's work, even though his *Science* papers had not yet been published.

NIH had one important item of business to accomplish before such an announcement took place. Neither Gallo's nor Montagnier's laboratory yet had a patent on its blood test in the United States, and the winner of that prize stood to make a great deal of money from sales of the test to blood banks and physicians. Both knew that the law required them to submit their applications for a patent before publishing the details of their tests. The Institut Pasteur had applied for a U.S. patent in mid-September 1983, and a patent attorney working for NIH hastily did the same for Gallo's test on the morning of April 23, the proposed date for Heckler's speech. The NIH patent application did not mention, as it should have done, that the French had already asked for a patent on a very similar test.

At 1:00 P.M. on April 23, 1984, Margaret Heckler took the podium at a national press conference and proudly announced:

Margaret Heckler, secretary of the federal Department of Health and Human Services, announced at a press conference in Washington, D.C., on April 23, 1984, that Robert Gallo had discovered the probable cause of AIDS, a virus that he called HTLV-3. She angered Luc Montagnier and others in his laboratory by making little or no mention of the French group's contribution to this landmark discovery. Heckler (*left*) is shown here at the press conference with Gallo. (*AP Images*)

> The probable cause of AIDS has been found—a variant of a known human cancer virus, called HTLV-3. . . . In particular, credit must go to our eminent Dr. Robert Gallo, . . . who directed the research that produced this discovery. . . . Today, we add another miracle to the long honor roll of American medicine and science.

Heckler also said that Gallo's laboratory had developed a test that would identify the virus in individuals and in samples of donated blood. With that test, she said, "We can identify AIDS victims with essentially 100 percent certainty. Thus, we should be able to ensure that blood for transfusion is free from AIDS [virus]." Heckler even predicted optimistically that a vaccine against the terrible disease would be created within the next two years.

The written draft of Heckler's statement contained a paragraph pointing out that French researchers had also isolated the virus and praising their work. Robert Gallo quoted this paragraph in his autobiography:

> As is so often the case in scientific pursuit, other discoveries have occurred in different laboratories—even in different parts of the world—which will ultimately contribute to the goal we all seek: the conquest of AIDS. I especially want to cite the efforts of the Pasteur Institute in France, which has in part been working in collaboration with the National Cancer Institute. They have previously identified a virus which they have linked to AIDS patients, and within the next few weeks we will know with certainty whether that virus is the same one identified through NCI's work. We believe it will prove to be the same.

Accounts differ, however, about whether Heckler actually spoke these words. Gallo implies that she did, but Montagnier wrote in *Virus* that the HHS secretary "lost her voice at an unfortunate moment" and therefore never gave this public acknowledgment to the French. Gallo answered questions from the press after Heckler's speech ended, and (according to Steve Connor and Sharon Kingman's book, *The Search for the Virus*) when a reporter asked whether Gallo's HTLV-3 was the same as the French LAV, Gallo replied only, "If it turns out to be the same I certainly will say so . . . [but] I cannot say at this point whether the two viruses are identical." Not surprisingly, Luc Montagnier and the other members of his laboratory were furious that this world-shaking announcement had acknowledged their contributions to the AIDS virus discovery only briefly, if at all.

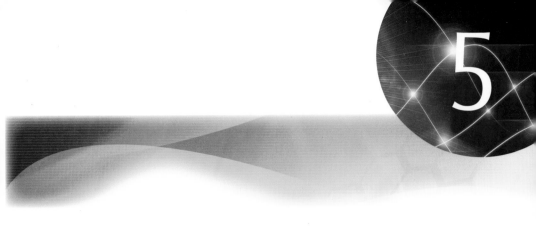

Struggle for Credit

No less than four papers by members of the Gallo laboratory appeared in the May 4, 1984, *Science,* the most from a single laboratory ever to be published in one issue. All trumpeted Robert Gallo's discovery of HTLV-3 and presented evidence that this virus causes AIDS. For instance, the group wrote, they found antibodies to HTLV-3 in almost 90 percent of AIDS patients and 80 percent of those with lymphadenopathy and other symptoms considered to be precursors to AIDS. Although Gallo and his coworkers pointed out differences between this virus and its cousins, HTLV-1 and HTLV-2, they emphasized that they considered all three viruses to be members of the same virus family.

COMPARING VIRUSES

Unlike the case in 1983, Luc Montagnier's team had no paper to accompany those by Gallo, and once again the summary news article published before the group of papers hardly mentioned the Pasteur group's work. That work, however, was very much on the minds of the retrovirologists and AIDS researchers who read the papers. Everyone wanted an answer to the question the reporter at the Heckler-Gallo press conference had asked: Were Gallo's HTLV-3 and Montagnier's LAV the same virus or not?

M. G. Sarngadharan, a researcher in Gallo's laboratory, brought a sample of HTLV-3 to Paris in mid-May so that the individual proteins in the two viruses could be compared. That comparison showed them to be similar, if not identical. So did a different type of test that Gallo's laboratory carried out, which compared *restriction maps* of the two viruses' genetic material. Scientists made these maps by treating a virus's nucleic acid with *restriction enzymes,* substances that bacteria make to protect themselves against attack by viruses. The enzymes cut the viruses' DNA or RNA into small pieces, thus preventing the viruses from reproducing. Each restriction enzyme slices a strand of nucleic acid whenever it encounters a particular sequence of bases, and enzymes from different bacteria make cuts at different sequences. If the genetic material from two viruses treated with the same enzymes produces groups of fragments with the same lengths, this is good evidence that the viruses are the same.

Gallo telephoned Montagnier in July to tell him that the restriction maps from the two viruses were almost exactly the same. According to Gallo's autobiography, Montagnier took the news calmly, saying only "They *should* be very close—they were all the same virus, after all." When Gallo went on to suggest that the maps matched because Montagnier's virus culture had somehow become contaminated with the virus that Sarngadharan had brought, however, Montagnier wrote in *Virus,* "If we had used videophones, he would have seen me literally leap out of my chair, on the verge of apoplexy." (Apoplexy is an old name for a stroke, which was once thought to be triggered by extreme anger.)

If any contamination had occurred, Montagnier insisted, it had to have happened earlier, in Gallo's own laboratory. For one thing, Montagnier told Gallo, he had sent a sample of LAV to another NIH scientist, Malcolm Martin, in April 1984—a month before Sarngadharan had brought Gallo's virus to the Institut Pasteur—and Martin had also found that LAV and HTLV-3 had identical restriction maps. For another, in order to prevent exactly the kind of accident Gallo was describing, Montagnier had kept Sarngadharan's culture in his own locked laboratory, which was in a different building from Chermann and Barré-Sinoussi's "Bru room." Finally, there had been no HTLV-3 from any source in Paris when the Pasteur group infected their B cell line the previous fall, and it was this culture that had provided the LAV used in the comparison tests.

CHANGEABLE GENES

Both Montagnier and Gallo knew that restriction maps could provide only an approximate comparison between the two viruses. The only way to find

Flossie Wong-Staal, a key member of Robert Gallo's laboratory in the 1980s, led the team that determined the base sequence of the Gallo virus's genome. She also played an important part in learning about the virus's proteins. Gallo's autobiography quotes her as saying "Working with this virus is like putting your hand in a treasure chest. Every time you put your hand in you pull out a gem." She is shown here at the 10th International Conference on AIDS in 1994. (*Dr. Flossie Wong-Staal*)

out once and for all whether the viruses were the same was to determine the exact order of the approximately 9,000 bases in the viruses' genomes. Researchers can perform such a task (called *sequencing*) very quickly today, but it was a much more laborious process in 1984.

Both laboratories completed the sequences of their viruses' genomes in November 1984 and published them in different scientific journals within a few days of each other in January 1985. As with the restriction maps, the sequences were virtually identical, differing by only 87 bases out of 9,213. The sequences were also similar to those of other viruses in the lentivirus family, showing that the new virus clearly belonged in this family, just as Montagnier had claimed. "The sequence data was a shock to us," John Crewdson quotes Gallo as saying in 1990, because the data showed so clearly that the AIDS virus was not related to the HTLVs, as the NCI scientist had continued to believe.

The importance of this close match became even clearer a month or two later, when both laboratories sequenced viruses taken from AIDS patients in different places. Montagnier's group, for instance, compared the sequences

(*continues on page 58*)

RYAN WHITE (1971–1990): UNFAIR DISCRIMINATION

By the time Luc Montagnier and Robert Gallo identified the virus that causes AIDS, scientists who studied the disease had no doubt about how it was spread: through sex, through infected blood, and directly from mother to child. They were equally sure that it was *not* spread through the air (by coughing and sneezing) or by casual contact, such as shaking hands or sharing eating utensils or drinking glasses. This information was widely published, but many members of the public did not believe it. Blinded by fear and prejudice, they continued to shun people with AIDS.

One of the best-known victims of this treatment was Ryan White (1971–90), a middle school student from Kokomo, Indiana. White, a hemophiliac, was diagnosed with AIDS in 1984 after receiving contaminated blood products. Doctors at first expected White to die within a few months, but his condition improved, and in mid-1985 he asked to return to school. Parents and teachers protested, fearing that others at the

Prejudice and fear that AIDS could be spread by casual contact led to shunning and mistreatment of people with the disease during the epidemic's early days. Here, demonstrators protest on the steps of New York's City Hall in November 1985 as a city council committee considers legislation to bar students and teachers with AIDS from attending public schools. *(AP Images)*

school might contract the disease from the boy. On June 30, the school superintendent denied White permission to attend classes.

Angry at this treatment, White's parents sued the school. Their court battle lasted eight months, ending with victory for the family in April 1986. Even though the Centers for Disease Control and the Indiana state health commissioner had told the school that White posed no health risk, some parents remained unconvinced, and they withdrew their children from classes when White returned. The school forced White to eat with disposable utensils and use a separate bathroom, and he and his family received death threats. In 1987, the family moved to Cicero, Indiana, where White attended high school and received much better treatment.

Ryan White, shown here, became a poster boy in the fight to stop discrimination against people with AIDS. When school officials tried to bar White, who had caught the disease through a blood transfusion, from returning to classes, his parents sued the school. They won, but continuing prejudice made White's life miserable until he and his family moved to a different town. (*AP Images*)

White's story was widely publicized and drew national attention to the mistreatment of people with AIDS. White himself frequently appeared on television programs, and he spoke to President Ronald Reagan's commission on AIDS in 1988. White emphasized that education about AIDS had made the difference between the public attitude in Kokomo and that in Cicero.

(*continues*)

(continued)

Ryan White died of AIDS complications on April 8, 1990. His experiences inspired a number of private AIDS charities, including one founded by his mother. In August 1990, furthermore, Congress passed the Ryan White Comprehensive AIDS Resources Emergency Act, usually called the Ryan White CARE Act. This act, which has been renewed several times, most recently in 2009, funds the largest federal program providing treatment and other forms of help for people with HIV/AIDS.

(continued from page 55)

of viruses taken from two patients from Zaire with each other, with the LAV growing in the Pasteur laboratory, and with the sequence of the virus that Jay Levy had isolated in California. The groups found that although all the sequences had enough similarities to show that they came from the same kind of virus, they also varied from person to person and place to place. The sequences were even different in samples of virus taken from the same patient at different times. The only exception was the comparison between Gallo's main virus isolate (the one growing in Mika Popovic's cell line and being used in the Gallo laboratory's ELISA test), which he called *HTLV-3B*, and Montagnier's LAV. According to Steve Connor and Sharon Kingman's *The Search for the Virus,* the sequences of LAV and HTLV-3B differed only by about 1 percent, whereas they differed from the other three virus isolates Montagnier tested by 10 to 20 percent or more.

Gallo's explanation for the similarity was that the unknown patient from which HTLV-3B had come and the donor of Montagnier's LAV must have become infected at the same time and place, probably New York City; one man might even have infected the other. Montagnier said that this could not be so, however, because Frédéric Brugière had not visited New York since 1979, whereas Gallo's blood samples all dated from late 1982 or early 1983. A later comparison of viruses taken from the donor and recipient of a virus-contaminated blood transfusion two years after the transfusion had taken place suggested that even if one man had infected the other in 1979, the sequences of their viruses would have differed by 5 to 10 percent several years later. It was far more likely, Montagnier claimed, that one of the two sets of LAV samples that he had sent to Gallo in 1983 had somehow contaminated the NCI laboratory's cultures and had then been reisolated as HTLV-3B.

The many variations in sequence that Montagnier's, Gallo's, and other laboratories detected in AIDS virus samples from different people in early 1985 did more than add to the puzzle of the relationship between Montagnier's virus and Gallo's. The variations suggested that this virus's genetic material, especially the gene carrying the instructions for making the virus's protein envelope, mutates much more often than that of most other viruses. Part of the changes, researchers learned later, come from the fact that the AIDS virus's reverse transcriptase frequently makes mistakes when it copies the viral RNA into the DNA of the cells that the virus infects.

The virus's high mutation rate was discouraging news to scientists involved in AIDS research because it meant that developing either vaccines or drugs to combat the illness would be exceptionally difficult. The antibodies in a vaccine have to match and attach to particular proteins in a virus or other microorganism. If the microbe's genes mutate, the proteins for which those genes carry the instructions will also become slightly different. The antibodies that fitted the old version of the proteins will not "recognize" the new version, so the vaccine will no longer provide protection against that microbe. In essence, the vaccine faces the same problem as a police officer trying to capture criminals who constantly change their names and alter their appearance with disguises. If a virus or other microbe has a high rate of mutation, it is also more likely to develop a new form that can resist a particular drug than a microbe whose genes seldom change.

A LESS-THAN-PERFECT TEST

While Luc Montagnier, Robert Gallo, and other scientists were learning more about the deadly virus they had discovered, others were converting the two laboratories' ELISA tests into a commercial form that could be used for widespread screening in blood banks and doctors' offices. In June 1984, the Department of Health and Human Services (HHS) granted licenses to Abbott Laboratories, a large pharmaceutical firm that specialized in diagnostic blood tests, and four other competing drug companies to develop a commercial test for antibodies to Gallo's HTLV-3B. The Institut Pasteur made a similar arrangement with Genetic Systems, a small biotechnology company in Seattle, Washington, a month or so later.

Before any drug, test, or other medical treatment can be sold in the United States, the federal Food and Drug Administration (FDA) must certify, based on information provided by the company that manufactures the treatment, that the treatment is both safe and effective in human beings. Obtaining FDA approval for a new treatment often takes years, but, responding to growing anxiety about the safety of the U.S. blood supply, the FDA granted approval for Abbott's AIDS blood test kit in record time. The kit began to be sold in March 1985. Both blood banks and individuals eager to know whether they carried the virus greeted the new test with enthusiasm, but problems soon began to appear. The test proved to generate a number of both false positives and false negatives.

A *false positive* test result states that antibodies to the AIDS virus are present in a blood sample when no such antibodies are actually there. False positives were a problem for blood banks because they forced the banks to discard units of perfectly healthy blood—and blood was always in short supply. Such results created far worse troubles for individuals. To begin with, a person who received a false positive test result was frightened into believing, incorrectly, that he or she had a life-threatening disease. Furthermore, because of the irrational fears that the public still had about AIDS, people whose test results became known might be rejected by family and friends or even lose jobs, homes, or health insurance. Positive results were usually checked with a more complex and expensive but more accurate test called the Western blot, but even this test was not completely foolproof.

A *false negative* test result created even more serious problems. Such a result fails to reveal antibodies to the virus, even though the antibodies— and the virus—are present in the sample. Researchers learned in mid-1986 that false negatives often occurred when people were tested soon after they became infected. Only antibodies to a single viral protein, called p24, were formed at this early stage, and the Abbott test did not detect antibodies to p24. As a result, the test allowed some units of infected blood and organs for transplant to slip through its net. The individuals who donated them showed no sign of illness, so no one was aware of the danger—until the recipients of the tainted blood or organs developed AIDS months or years later. A number of cases of AIDS transmitted in this way were uncovered in the mid-1980s, after blood testing became widespread.

In mid-November 1985, the American Red Cross tested thousands of blood samples with both the Abbott test and and the Genetic Systems test. The Genetic Systems kit produced far fewer false positives and false negatives than the Abbott one. The Red Cross could not change tests at that time, however, because the FDA had not yet approved the Genetic Systems test for sale in the United States. It finally did so in February 1986.

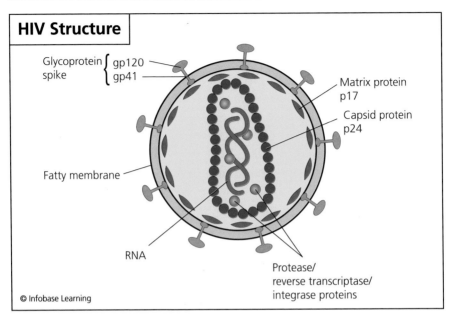

HIV Structure

Glycoprotein spike { gp120
gp41

Matrix protein p17

Capsid protein p24

Fatty membrane

RNA

Protease/ reverse transcriptase/ integrase proteins

© Infobase Learning

People infected with the HIV, the AIDS virus, form antibodies against different virus proteins at different times after infection. Early in infection, they have antibodies only to p24, the so-called capsid protein. The first ELISA test for antibodies to the virus could not detect antibodies to p24, so some infected blood samples were not identified.

PATENT BATTLE

While Abbott and Genetic Systems battled for a share of the blood test market, the institutions from whom the tests had come were engaging in an increasingly ugly struggle over ownership of the patent rights to the tests. Patent ownership was bound to produce a substantial amount of income from royalties, the share of money from sales of a product that is paid to the product's inventor or creator. Since the Gallo laboratory was part of the U.S. National Institutes of Health, and the French government similarly contributed to and received money from the Institut Pasteur, the governments of the two countries also stood to gain or lose money and prestige depending on the outcome of the battle. Luc Montagnier and Robert Gallo were not sure whether they would receive money from the patent, but they knew that the patent decision was bound to affect their scientific reputations and the degree of credit that each would receive for discovering the AIDS virus.

The U.S. Patent and Trademark Office awarded Gallo's laboratory a patent on its version of the ELISA test for the AIDS virus in May 1985. The patent *(continues on page 64)*

DOES HIV REALLY CAUSE AIDS?

Most scientists quickly accepted the evidence provided by Luc Montagnier, Robert Gallo, and others that the virus they had identified, later known as HIV, causes AIDS—but some did not, and a few still deny this link. The best known of the AIDS denialists is Peter H. Duesberg, a German-born professor of molecular and cell biology at the University of California, Berkeley, who gained fame in 1970 when he identified the first oncogene, *src*.

Beginning in 1987, Duesberg and his followers maintained that HIV has not been conclusively proven to cause AIDS. HIV has never been found in some people with conditions labeled as AIDS, they say, and conversely, some HIV-positive people do not develop AIDS. Duesberg claims that AIDS is caused by recreational drug use and other lifestyle factors in developed countries and is simply a new name for the immune suppression caused by malnutrition and multiple infections in Africa and other developing areas. He believes that HIV is a harmless passenger virus.

Although some scientists have defended Duesberg's right to express his dissenting opinions, nearly all reject the views themselves. Respected research centers such as NIH's National Institute of Allergy and Infectious Diseases have published answers to the questions Duesberg raises and provided extensive evidence to support the idea that HIV causes AIDS. For instance, they say, new tests for HIV antibodies and for the virus itself, much more accurate than the tests available in the 1980s, have found HIV or antibodies to it in virtually every AIDS patient tested. (Other conditions can suppress the immune system, but they almost never produce the loss of CD4 lymphocytes that is considered characteristic of AIDS.) More conclusively still, three laboratory workers who had no other risk factors for AIDS developed the disease after being accidentally exposed to purified, cloned HIV, and HIV was later isolated from their bodies and shown by genetic sequencing to match the specific virus to which they had been exposed.

Conversely, people without HIV infection do not develop AIDS (although they may suffer other forms of immune suppression). In some twin babies born to HIV-infected mothers, one baby in the pair tested positive for HIV and one did not. The HIV-positive infant developed AIDS, but the HIV-negative child remained healthy.

Duesberg's ideas do not explain the many cases of AIDS in people who have never used drugs, nor the fact that drug users who remain free of HIV infection do not develop the disease, critics point out. The high death rate from AIDS among young, formerly healthy middle-class adults

(continues)

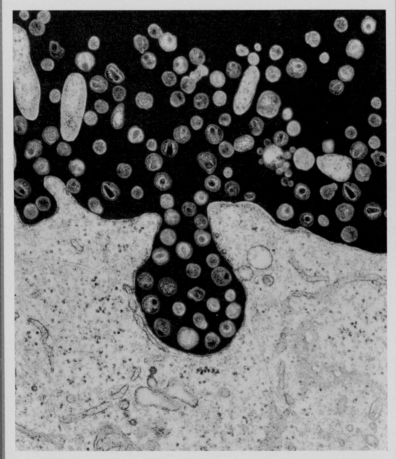

This color-enhanced transmission electron micrograph shows HIV particles bursting out of an infected T lymphocyte. Some critics have claimed that HIV does not really cause AIDS, but most scientists reject their arguments. *(Hans Gelderblom/Stone/Getty Images)*

(continued)

in Africa also does not fit his theory. Finally, if AIDS were not due to HIV— or at least to some form of retrovirus—antiretroviral drugs would not be able to control the illness, as they have been shown to do in many cases.

Supporters of the idea that HIV causes AIDS have stressed that the views of the AIDS denialists can be dangerous when they persuade people that they can safely indulge in behavior that puts them at risk for HIV infection or when they keep people from seeking drug treatment when they show symptoms of AIDS. On a larger scale, Thabo Mbeki (1942–   ), president of South Africa from 1999 to 2008, used AIDS denialism as a reason for not starting AIDS treatment programs in that country, and public health researchers in South Africa and at Harvard University estimated that as many as 340,000 unnecessary deaths and 171,000 new HIV infections resulted from this policy. Barbara Hogan, the health minister appointed by Mbeki's successor, was quoted in a 2008 *New York Times* article as saying, "The era of [AIDS] denialism is over completely in South Africa."

(continued from page 61)

office had not yet granted the Pasteur group a patent for its test, however, even though the institute had filed an application several months before NIH. Lawyers representing Pasteur threatened to sue the U.S. government if the institute's patent was not quickly granted. As ill feeling about the issue intensified in late 1985, both Montagnier and Gallo found themselves increasingly entangled in their institutions' and governments' claims and counterclaims. Both wrote later that they wished they could have avoided that involvement, which took time away from their AIDS research. However, in an interview with a reporter from *Paris Match,* Montagnier added, "But it is a question of principles, a question of ethics. If France does not do anything, it means that there is a group, across the Atlantic, which is above the laws." The two men also saw the patent dispute as a larger echo of their own personal feud about which laboratory had been the first to discover the AIDS virus.

NIH and Pasteur officials, and sometimes Montagnier and Gallo as well, attempted to settle the patent question without going to court, but they were unsuccessful. In mid-November 1985, a U.S. law firm acting for Pasteur asked the U.S. Patent and Trademark Office to declare an interference with the Gallo patent. (John Crewdson defines an interference as "an administrative proceeding intended to sort out competing [patent] claims.") Before the patent office could rule on this request, the institute sued the U.S. government in a Washington, D.C., claims court on December 12, asking for recognition of the Pasteur group as the first to discover the virus and as independent inventors of the blood test, as well as a share of the patent royalties for the U.S. blood test.

A SECOND AIDS VIRUS

While lawyers for NIH and Pasteur prepared to do battle, Luc Montagnier's laboratory found a vital clue to the AIDS virus's origin: a second virus, enough unlike LAV to be classified as a different "species," yet clearly related. The viruses' core proteins were similar, but the proteins in their envelopes were so different that antibodies to LAV envelope proteins did not react with those in the new virus. The Pasteur scientists first saw this virus in fall 1984 in the blood of patients that a visiting physician had brought from Lisbon, Portugal. The patients had come originally from Guinea-Bissau, a former Portuguese colony in West Africa. They had all the symptoms of AIDS and their blood tested positive for reverse transcriptase, but they did not have antibodies to LAV. Montagnier published a paper about his group's discovery in January 1986.

Montagnier's laboratory worked out the genetic sequence of the new virus shortly thereafter and found that it shared only 42 percent of that sequence with LAV. The virus proved to be closely related to retroviruses that had been found in two kinds of African monkeys. This supported the idea, which many scientists studying AIDS had held for some years, that the AIDS virus had originated in Africa as a monkey or ape virus that mutated in a way that allowed it to infect humans.

INVESTIGATIONS OF THE PAST

The outcome of both the patent suit and the dispute about credit for discovering the AIDS virus and developing the blood test depended on determining the exact sequence of events in the Gallo and Montagnier laboratories, especially Gallo's, during late 1982 and 1983. Pasteur lawyers repeatedly interviewed Gallo, Mika Popovic, and other scientists in the Gallo laboratory in early 1986, but the scientists' statements were sometimes contradictory. The lawyers also collected boxes of notebooks, letters, and other

documents from the laboratory, but these, too, were so confusing that a clear chronology could not be assembled.

Some of the facts that did come to light did not seem to reflect well on Gallo. For instance, following an anonymous lead, James Swire, the Institut Pasteur's chief lawyer in the patent case, discovered that a virus photograph in one of the laboratory's May 1984 *Science* articles had been labeled HTLV-3 but in fact was a photo of LAV that Matthew Gonda had taken in December 1983. Gallo published a short letter in the April 18, 1986, *Science* in which he admitted this mistake. He said that it had occurred accidentally and was not important, but an accompanying news article in the magazine remarked that Gallo's admission was "likely to raise a few eyebrows" and "could also have some legal ramifications" for the patent dispute. Some scientists and science writers saw the error as evidence that Gallo's claims could not be trusted.

One issue that had divided the Montagnier and Gallo laboratories—the name to be used for the AIDS virus—was finally settled in May 1986. An international committee headed by Harold Varmus, one of the two scientists who had shown that cancer-causing genes were mutated forms of normal cell genes, decided that the virus would be known as HIV, short for human immunodeficiency virus. The new virus that Montagnier's group had found in West Africa became HIV-2.

The U.S. patent office, meanwhile, seemed to be leaning toward the French side of the patent quarrel. In the same month that the AIDS virus acquired its new name, the office granted Pasteur's request for an interference with the Gallo patent and made Pasteur the "senior party" in the patent dispute. This meant that the U.S. government, rather than the French institute, had the responsibility of proving that the patent for the U.S. AIDS blood test should belong to them.

A LANDMARK AGREEMENT

By late 1986, the charges and countercharges in the patent and credit disputes had grown so vicious that many observers felt that the quarrel was damaging the reputation of science as a whole. "The whole thing was sordid," Claudine Escoffier, medical editor of the influential French newspaper *Le Monde,* said

(opposite page) During the mid-1980s, Luc Montagnier and Robert Gallo continued to argue about whether the virus that Gallo called HTLV-3 and the one that Montagnier called LAV were the same. Montagnier is shown here in his office at the Institut Pasteur in 1984 with pictures of Gallo's virus (top) and his own (bottom). The viruses later proved to be identical. *(AP Images)*

later, according to John Crewdson's *Science Fictions*. "Millions of dollars were spent on both sides to pay lawyers. It would have been much better to invest them in science." A group of Nobel laureates sent an open letter to newly reelected U.S. president Ronald Reagan (1911–2004) in November 1986 urging him to "bring the power of your office, your wisdom, and your humanity to bear in helping to achieve a solution" to the argument. "Given the grave crisis which AIDS presents, it does not befit the scientific community to be engaged in what appears to be a self-serving dispute."

Jonas Salk (1914–95), who had invented the first polio vaccine in 1952 and was now a sort of elder statesman of science, tried to mediate a settlement between the two laboratories. Partly at his urging, Gallo and Montagnier met in Frankfurt, Germany, in late March 1987 to attempt to work out a mutually agreeable chronology of events related to the discovery of HIV.

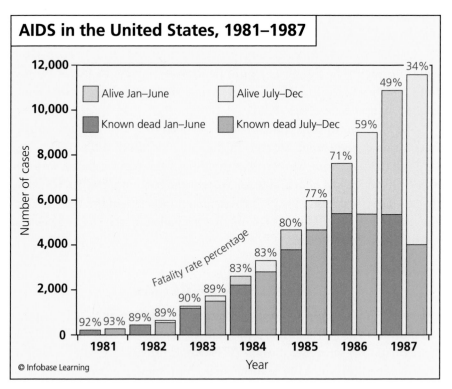

The number of AIDS cases in the United States rose steadily from 1981, when the illness was first reported, to 1987. Many scientists felt that the longstanding credit dispute between Luc Montagnier and Robert Gallo, which eventually extended to their institutions and even their countries' governments, was a shameful distraction at a time when research on this deadly disease was so badly needed.

The dispute between the National Institutes of Health and the Institut Pasteur over rights to the AIDS blood test was finally settled by an international agreement ratified by the heads of the U.S. and French governments on March 31, 1987. Here, French prime minister Jacques Chirac applauds U.S. president Ronald Reagan during ratification ceremonies at the White House. *(AP Images)*

Their work, published in *Nature* on April 2, bolstered that of institute and government officials, who by this time were also eager for a settlement.

On March 31, 1987, the directors of NIH and the Institut Pasteur signed an agreement intended to end the legal case and the disputes behind it once and for all. President Reagan and French premier Jacques Chirac (1932–   ) ratified the agreement in a ceremony at the White House. The agreement assigned the patents for both blood tests (the Institut Pasteur had finally won a U.S. patent for its test a few weeks earlier) to both institutions and their leading scientists and awarded each institution an equal share of the patent royalties. Eighty percent of the royalties, however, would go to a new world foundation for AIDS research, whose trustees would come from both Pasteur and HHS. A quarter of the foundation's money would be applied to research on AIDS in the developing world, especially Africa.

NEW HOPE FOR AIDS SUFFERERS

News media hailed the settlement of the patent dispute, but they had brought far more important news to those suffering from AIDS and their loved ones the previous fall: the first treatment that showed real promise against the disease. NCI researcher Samuel Broder and scientists at the U.S. facility of Burroughs Wellcome (now GlaxoSmithKline), a large British-based drug firm, had begun a search for anti-AIDS drugs in 1984. After testing a number of possibilities, they found that a compound called *azidothymidine*, or *AZT* for short, stopped HIV from killing T cells in laboratory cultures.

AZT is chemically very similar to thymidine, one of the bases in DNA. When HIV uses reverse transcriptase to copy its genetic RNA into DNA and AZT is present, the enzyme mistakenly attaches an AZT molecule to the growing DNA chain in place of thymidine. AZT is different enough from thymidine to keep other bases from attaching to it as they would to thymidine. As a result, once AZT joins a DNA chain, the reverse transcriptase cannot continue building the chain, and the virus therefore cannot reproduce. (AZT affects normal DNA reproduction in cells, too, but reverse transcriptase is much more sensitive to it than cellular copying enzymes are.)

Following the usual pattern for developing new medicines, Burroughs Wellcome next tested AZT on animals to determine how toxic (poisonous) it was. The toxicity did not appear to be great, so in summer 1985 they gave it to 20 desperately ill AIDS patient. Most of them improved, and for two, the

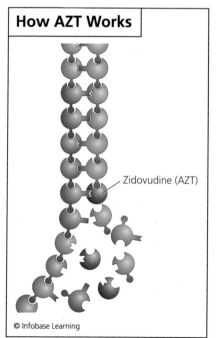

How AZT Works

Zidovudine (AZT)

© Infobase Learning

Azidothymidine, or AZT (also called zidovudine), resembles thymidine, one of the four bases in DNA. The difference between them is great enough, however, to keep HIV's reverse transcriptase from being able to continue making a chain of DNA after the enzyme has added a molecule of AZT to the chain in place of a thymidine molecule. As a result, the virus cannot reproduce.

drug offered a seemingly miraculous "resurrection," restoring them from a state near death to apparently perfect health.

The next round of AZT tests, begun in February 1986, involved 281 people with AIDS from various parts of the country. Half of them received AZT and the other half an inactive sugar pill, called a *placebo*. Neither the patients nor their doctors knew which substance each person was taking. Researchers use this kind of *double-blind test* in drug development because sick people's health often improves simply because they know they are receiving a new medication, even if the pill they take contains no active ingredients. On September 11, however, the effectiveness of AZT, as compared to the placebo, had become so clear that FDA officials stopped the double-blind test and began allowing AZT to be distributed to physicians and patients around the country.

AZT did not cure AIDS, but by early 1987, when Reagan and Chirac finally signed the agreement intended to end the quarrel between Luc Montagnier and Robert Gallo's laboratories, the disease's sufferers and their doctors were beginning to feel hope, an emotion that had previously eluded them. As one such physician, Paul Volberding, put it in an interview with Dominique Lapierre, "For the first time, we were going to be able to do something other than stand by and watch our patients die."

The Ultimate Prize

At first, the arguments surrounding the discovery of the AIDS virus seemed to be over. For one thing, the settlement signed by Reagan and Chirac forbade any of the scientists involved to publicly discuss or challenge the agreement. Both Luc Montagnier and Robert Gallo returned to their laboratories, intent on seeking a treatment or vaccine for the deadly virus they had discovered. They shared several major awards, including the (U.S.) Lasker Award for Basic Medical Research in 1986, Canada's Gairdner Prize in 1987, and Japan's Science and Technology Prize (called the Japan Prize for short) in 1988.

INVESTIGATIONS AND DISCOVERIES

Beneath the placid surface established by the Reagan-Chirac agreement, however, anger still smoldered. Some of it surfaced within Montagnier's own laboratory. Jean-Claude Chermann and Françoise Barré-Sinoussi both left the laboratory in late 1987, partly because they felt that, just as Gallo had seemingly tried to deny credit to Montagnier, Montagnier in turn had not given them enough credit for their roles in HIV's discovery. "When we start, it was the virus of Barré, Chermann, Montagnier," John Crewdson quotes Chermann as saying shortly after Chermann's departure from the Institut Pasteur. "The following year it was Montagnier, Chermann, Barré. Then it was 'the team of Pasteur.' Now it's Montagnier." Chermann told Crewdson that his main reason for leaving, however, was that the Institut Pasteur had failed to give him a promotion that he had hoped for. He moved to Marseilles, while Barré-Sinoussi transferred to a different department within the institute. Pasteur's managers were more generous to Montagnier, giving him a whole floor in the institute's new retrovirology building in 1991 and putting him in charge of a new department of AIDS and retroviruses at the same time.

In the early 1990s, Robert Gallo once again found his and his teammates' behavior during the key months of the HIV discovery placed under a microscope. John Crewdson, a Pulitzer Prize-winning investigative reporter for the *Chicago Tribune,* published a long article in that newspaper on November 19, 1989, claiming that Gallo's HTLV-3B was Montagnier's LAV by another name. "What happened in Robert Gallo's lab during the winter of 1983–1984 is a mystery that may never be entirely solved. But the evidence is compelling that [the identity of the two viruses resulted from] either an accident or a theft," Crewdson wrote. In a follow-up article, the reporter suggested that some of the statements that representatives of NIH and the Department of Health and Human Services, as well as Gallo and other NCI scientists, had made in court and before the patent office had been untrue.

Gallo denied all of Crewdson's charges, but a copy of Crewdson's long article fell into the hands of John D. Dingell (D-Mich., 1926–   ), who was then in charge of the powerful House Energy and Commerce Committee. This committee included a subcommittee on oversight and investigations, which began examining high-profile cases of alleged scientific fraud in April 1988. After reading the *Tribune* article, Dingell pressured NIH to look into Crewdson's accusations, and NIH in turn assigned the investigation to its Office of Scientific Integrity (OSI), a body that was supposed to investigate charges of scientific misconduct leveled against NIH scientists. The inquiry, which passed through several agencies, began in January 1990 and continued for four years.

Meanwhile, Luc Montagnier continued to study HIV and its effects on cells. In 1990, he hypothesized that *mycoplasma,* a type of small bacterium that can cause pneumonia and other diseases, might be a necessary *cofactor* in producing AIDS. Infection with HIV resulted in AIDS, he believed, only if mycoplasma were also present. This idea is controversial, but Montagnier still believes that infection with mycoplasma or other small bacteria may make HIV infection worse.

Montagnier's laboratory made a more significant discovery in 1991. Rather than killing T cells directly, his group found, HIV activates a genetic program that makes the cells destroy themselves. This "cell suicide," called *apoptosis,* is a normal and often useful mechanism; for instance, certain genes trigger it when they detect changes in other genes that are likely to make the cell become cancerous. Apoptosis is also part of the functioning of a healthy immune system. When an infection occurs, the system manufactures numerous cells to attack the invading microorganisms. These cells are no longer necessary after the infection is controlled, so the apoptosis program tells them to self-destruct. Somehow HIV turns on the program at the wrong time, leading to the destruction of most of the body's T cells. The Pasteur group also showed that the AIDS virus stresses, and therefore weakens, the immune system by triggering certain harmful chemical reactions and by keeping the system constantly activated.

A SURPRISE CONTAMINATION

Also in 1991, the investigation into Robert Gallo's conduct shed new light on events that had occurred in Montagnier's own laboratory during the crucial early years of work on HIV. Attempting to refute the charge that LAV had contaminated his virus cultures, Gallo ordered members of his laboratory to sequence a sample of the virus that Montagnier had brought to the United States in July 1983. He published a short note in *Nature* on February 28, 1991, coauthored by Chermann, stating that the base sequence of this virus did not match the sequence that Simon Wain-Hobson, a member of Montagnier's research team, had published for LAV-Bru in January 1985—the sequence that had been shown to match almost completely the sequence of Gallo's HTLV-3B.

This finding shocked and puzzled Montagnier and his coworkers. After talking with Françoise Barré-Sinoussi, Wain-Hobson found that she had brought samples of virus from two different cultures to Gallo in September 1983. One was from the same culture as the sample that Montagnier had brought in July, but records from Gallo's laboratory showed that the other culture was the one used in that laboratory's later experiments.

Barré-Sinoussi's own notes showed that at that time her laboratory contained cultures of cells from three AIDS or pre-AIDS patients: Frédéric Brugière, Christophe Lailier, and Eric Loiseau. Wain-Hobson had sequenced the viruses from all these cultures earlier and found that the Lailier virus contained a short string of bases not present in viruses from the other two patients. When he reexamined his published sequence of what he had thought was the Bru virus—the one that had grown in Montagnier's B cell line—he found the telltale string there as well. In short, the virus whose sequence Wain-Hobson had published, and which matched the sequence of Gallo's HTLV-3B, was not really LAV-Bru at all. Instead, it was the Lailier virus, LAV-Lai, which Montagnier recalled had grown exceptionally well.

The mystery—or at least part of it—now appeared to be solved. In late July or early August 1983, LAV-Lai apparently had contaminated some of the LAV-Bru cultures, including the one that eventually grew in the B-cell line. Without knowing it, Barré-Sinoussi had brought a sample of one of these cultures to Gallo in September, and it had somehow found its way into Mika Popovic's virus pool. It was the only virus to survive and grow in the permanent cell line, at which point Gallo named it HTLV-3B. This reconstruction explained why LAV, as the Montagnier group knew it, and HTLV-3B were genetically all but identical, and yet, as Gallo correctly stated, LAV-Bru and HTLV-3B were different. It also meant that HTLV-3B was still a French virus, even if it was not the one that Montagnier and his coworkers had believed it to be. Wain-Hobson confirmed the picture when he sequenced virus from a sample of the second culture brought to Gallo, which Barré-Sinoussi unearthed from her freezer at his request. It, too, possessed the unique sequence that marked it as being LAV-Lai. "There is no doubt that Lai is the source of HTLV-3B," a news article in the May 10, 1991, *Science* quoted Wain-Hobson as saying.

In an article in the May 30, 1991, issue of *Nature*, Gallo finally admitted what he had so long denied: However the contamination might have come about, HTLV-3B, the strain of virus that his laboratory had used in developing their blood test, was one that Luc Montagnier's team at Pasteur had discovered first. Scientists at Roche Diagnostic Systems, a California subsidiary of the large Swiss pharmaceutical company Hoffman-La Roche, confirmed this conclusion later in 1991 when they reported on the results of genetic tests they had made on the candidate viruses using a new technique called *PCR (polymerase chain reaction),* which simplifies the analysis and comparison of small amounts of DNA. The Roche researchers stated that MOV, one of the virus isolates in Gallo's laboratory that contributed to the pool from which HTLV-3B emerged, was identical to LAV-Lai. The Roche group published their findings in *Nature* on June 3, 1993.

CHARGES DROPPED

The question of whether Robert Gallo or Mika Popovic was guilty of "scientific misconduct" proved to be far more complex. John Crewdson recounts the investigation of this issue in detail in *Science Fictions,* a long book that grew out of his newspaper article about Gallo. Rather than addressing the questions of exactly how LAV-Lai had become HTLV-3B and whether Popovic or Gallo was aware of the mislabeling at the time it had happened, the Office of Scientific Integrity and the several agencies that succeeded it focused on the narrower issue of the truth of several statements in Mika Popovic's May 1984 *Science* paper. Several times the investigators concluded that Popovic was guilty of scientific misconduct for falsifying these statements. In some cases, they also found Gallo guilty, primarily of failing in his duty as a laboratory chief by not supervising or checking Popovic's work carefully enough. However, responding (according to Crewdson) to pressure from high officials in NIH or the Department of Health and Human Services, the committees' final reports found Gallo innocent and withdrew most of the negative comments about him.

The Office of Research Integrity (ORI), which replaced the Office of Scientific Integrity, issued a report in December 1992 stating that Gallo and Popovic were guilty of misconduct, chiefly in regard to misstatements in Popovic's paper. However, an appeals board, the Research Integrity Adjudications Panel, reversed the guilty verdict against Popovic in November 1993 without a hearing. "One might anticipate . . . after all the sound and fury,

Czech-born Mikulas (Mika) Popovic, shown here, was an important researcher in Robert Gallo's laboratory during the laboratory's early research on AIDS. Investigative agencies convicted Popovic of scientific misconduct in the early 1990s because of misstatements in a key paper that he published in *Science* in 1984, but an appeals board reversed the conviction in 1993. *(Institute of Human Virology/ University of Maryland School of Medicine)*

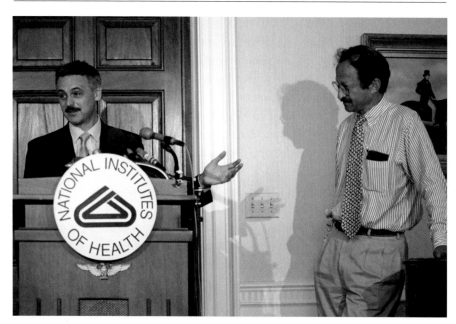

After new research revealed that the virus used in the Gallo laboratory's blood test for antibodies to HIV had actually originated in Luc Montagnier's laboratory, the patent royalties for the test were redistributed, with a larger share going to the Institut Pasteur. Here, Harold Varmus, director of the National Institutes of Health *(right)*, and Maxime Schwartz, director general of the Institut Pasteur, speak at a news conference at NIH announcing the revised patent settlement on July 11, 1994. *(AP Images)*

there would be at least a residue of palpable wrongdoing. That is not the case," Christine Gorman quoted the panel as saying in her article about the ruling in *Time* magazine on November 22, 1993.

A few days after the panel's acquittal of Popovic, the ORI dropped its charges against Gallo. "I have been completely vindicated," Gallo told reporters. A news article in the November 19, 1993, *Science,* however, quoted a statement from the ORI in which the agency said it took this action because the adjudications panel had told it that the panel would sustain the guilty verdicts only if the ORI could show that Popovic or Gallo had *intended* to be deceitful when they made incorrect statements and, furthermore, that their deceptions had had adverse effects on the scientific community—charges that would be almost impossible to prove. The ORI wrote that the panel's ruling "established a new definition of scientific misconduct as well as a new and extremely difficult standard for proving misconduct."

The Institut Pasteur and its lawyers did not care how the virus substitution had come about—only that it had occurred. As early as 1991, after they learned informally about the Office of Scientific Integrity's report and later the results from the Roche scientists' test, which strongly suggested that Gallo's laboratory had (even if accidentally) used a French virus as the basis for their blood test, they began demanding reimbursement of their legal fees in the patent case, back royalties, interest, and a greater share of future royalties on the test. By the fall of 1992, they were threatening to take the U.S. government to court once more if adjustments were not made.

The court case was never renewed, but on July 11, 1994, the French finally prevailed. The board of the French and American AIDS Foundation, the institution established to handle the patent royalties in the Reagan-Chirac settlement, agreed that Pasteur would receive 60 percent of the royalties divided between the two institutions. That sum was estimated to amount to $6 million over the following eight years. At the same time, the Department of Health and Human Services issued a public statement acknowledging that a French virus had been used in the American blood test.

NEW AIDS TREATMENTS

Despite the best efforts of Luc Montagnier, Robert Gallo, and the many other scientists around the world who were studying HIV and AIDS, the epidemic continued to advance during the 1990s. By 1992, AIDS was the leading cause of death of men between 24 and 44 years old in the United States, and a cure or a vaccine seemed as far away as ever. The Concorde trial, a large joint British-French test of AZT, showed in 1993 that this compound was far from the miracle drug that it had first appeared to be; HIV rapidly developed mutations that were resistant to the drug, so it did not slow the progression of AIDS for long. (AZT did prove to be effective, however, in breaking the chain of transmission between infected mothers and their unborn children.) The same problem arose with other drugs that were tried against the disease.

In 1992, doctors began to find some success in keeping AIDS at bay by treating infected people with a combination of antiviral drugs. The virus could not develop resistance to this multipronged attack, which struck it at several different points in its reproductive cycle, as easily as it could to single medications. Ability to treat the disease improved further around 1996, when a new class of anti-HIV drugs called *protease inhibitors* came into use. With these drugs and a new method of multidrug therapy called *HAART (highly active antiretroviral therapy),* many people in the developed world began to experience HIV infection as a chronic disease, like heart disease or diabetes, rather than an immediate death sentence. In 1997, thanks to these

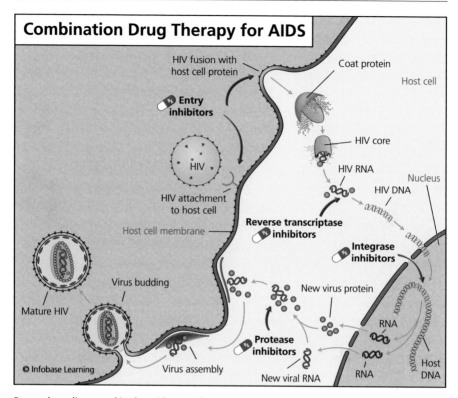

Combination Drug Therapy for AIDS

Researchers discovered in the mid-1990s that treatment combining three or more antiretroviral drugs was far more effective against HIV/AIDS than treatment with any one or even two drugs. The virus could not easily develop resistance to the treatment because the drugs were of different types, striking at different points in the virus's reproductive cycle. Entry inhibitors, for instance, keep the virus from entering cells. Reverse transcriptase inhibitors prevent HIV from copying its RNA into DNA. Integrase inhibitors keep the virus from integrating its DNA into the host cell's genome. Protease inhibitors stop it from making proteins for new viruses.

new treatments, the number of deaths from AIDS in the United States dropped substantially for the first time since the epidemic began.

Major problems remained, however. The new medications were extremely expensive, often caused *side effects* (unwanted effects of a medical treatment) that could range from annoying to life-threatening, and had to be taken throughout an infected person's life in order to keep the virus from multiplying. Treatment usually prevented the development of full-blown AIDS, but the wily virus still sometimes produced mutants that could evade all the drugs. More effective testing of the blood supply and education about ways to prevent exposure to HIV also began to lower the rate of infection in the United States and other developed countries in the 1990s—for awhile, at least. Some people were unwilling or unable to alter the behaviors that put them at risk for HIV infection, so the disease continued to spread, especially among African Americans and, later, Hispanics. The drop in new infections began to level off in the late 1990s.

DISASTER IN DEVELOPING COUNTRIES

The AIDS epidemic was far worse in developing countries, where the disease had spread like wildfire through sexual (chiefly heterosexual) transmission, sharing of needles by intravenous drug users, and tainted blood transfusions or medical instruments. Sub-Saharan Africa, where the illness was often called *slim* because one of its chief symptoms was sudden weight loss, had been hit first and hardest. AIDS spread both east and west from the Congo in the 1980s, following the travel paths of migrants (truck drivers, soldiers, miners, and others) and the female sex workers with whom they often associated. "In some towns [in central Africa around 1989], a fifth of the population was either dead or dying, and virtually every family had lost a member," Jonathan Engel wrote in *The Epidemic.* The focus of the disease moved to southern Africa at the end of the decade. In the early 1990s, numerous cases also began to appear in Asia, especially among users of heroin and other intravenous drugs.

In addition, many AIDS sufferers in the developing world were also infected by *tuberculosis,* a disease caused by bacteria that chiefly affects the lungs. Arata Kochi, manager of the World Health Organization's tuberculosis program, stated in 1995, "TB [tuberculosis] and HIV are feeding off each other at an alarming rate. When they're together, they multiply each other's impact."

The World Health Organization (WHO) estimated that there were more than 2.5 million cases of AIDS worldwide in 1993, and more than 14 million people were infected with HIV. Most were in the developing world, and almost none of them could afford the new antiviral drugs. Their countries also lacked the medical personnel and equipment needed to administer the drugs.

AIDS's threat to world health, social stability, and economy spawned numerous international organizations to help the countries most affected. Luc Montagnier and Federico Mayor, the former director general of the United Nations Educational, Scientific and Cultural Organization (UNESCO), founded one such organization, the World Foundation for AIDS Research and Prevention, in 1993 under the sponsorship of UNESCO. Montagnier is still president of the foundation, which has its headquarters in Paris. According to the foundation's Web site, its activities are "research and prevention [of HIV infection and AIDS], exchanges with other laboratories and research centres and with universities." It accomplishes these aims by establishing AIDS research and prevention centers, which it has now set up in more than eight countries. Montagnier cofounded a center in Abidjan, capital of the Ivory Coast (Côte d'Ivoire) in West Africa, in 1996, and later founded a similar center in a second African country, Cameroon.

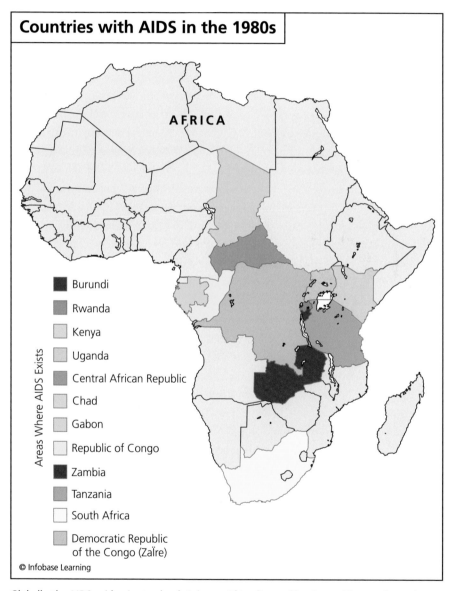

Countries with AIDS in the 1980s

AFRICA

Areas Where AIDS Exists

- Burundi
- Rwanda
- Kenya
- Uganda
- Central African Republic
- Chad
- Gabon
- Republic of Congo
- Zambia
- Tanzania
- South Africa
- Democratic Republic of the Congo (Zaïre)

© Infobase Learning

Globally, the AIDS epidemic struck sub-Saharan Africa first and hardest—this map shows the African countries with the highest numbers of HIV/AIDS cases in the 1980s.

THE ORIGIN OF HIV

Soon after Luc Montagnier and his coworkers discovered HIV, he and other researchers began to suspect that AIDS was one of many diseases that had originated in animals and spread to humans. (Influenza [flu] and bubonic plague [Black Death] are other human illnesses that came from animals.) Virologists knew of several *simian immunodeficiency viruses (SIVs)*, viruses genetically similar to HIV that infect different kinds of African monkeys, and they guessed that one of these might have mutated into HIV.

This theory gained support in 1999, when Paul Sharp and Beatrice Hahn discovered a virus related to SIV and HIV that infects chimpanzees, which are more closely related to humans than monkeys are. In particular, it infects a subspecies of chimpanzee that lives in west-central Africa, which many researchers believe is the most likely place for HIV to have originated. (These chimpanzees are now classified as endangered, but they were common in earlier times.) This virus is almost identical to HIV-1, the virus responsible for most cases of AIDS. In 2003, the same researchers stated that the chimpanzee virus, in turn, may have arisen when two SIVs, one that normally lived in red-capped mangabeys and one that lived in greater spot-nosed monkeys, infected chimpanzees at the same time and combined their genetic material while in their new hosts. The chimpanzees probably picked up the viruses when they hunted and ate infected monkeys.

Similarly, scientists have found that HIV-2 is essentially identical to an SIV that infects the sooty mangabey, or white-collared monkey. This monkey is native to West Africa, the area in which HIV-2 is usually found. A group of Belgian researchers concluded in 2003 that this virus passed to humans in the early 1940s in the West African country now called Guinea-Bissau (formerly Portuguese Guinea).

No one knows exactly when these viruses or closely related ones became able to infect humans, but researchers have guessed that this probably happened in the late 19th or early 20th centuries. Africans in remote areas hunt chimpanzees and monkeys as bush meat, and people may have become infected when blood from butchered animals entered open wounds or sores on their skin. Alternatively, infection may have occurred when monkeys or apes scratched or bit humans. This most likely happened several times, producing different strains of HIV.

NEW PLACES, NEW APPROACHES

The mid-1990s brought major changes for both Luc Montagnier and Robert Gallo. In 1996, Gallo left the National Cancer Institute and founded the Institute for Human Virology at the University of Maryland in Baltimore, a facility he still directs. Queens College, part of the City University of New York, offered Montagnier a similar opportunity in 1997. Montagnier retired from the Institut Pasteur at this time, though he still maintained a laboratory in the institute and spent part of his time in Paris. During Montagnier's years at the Flushing campus of Queens College, he continued to study the mechanisms by which HIV destroys T cells and the role of microorganisms such as mycoplasma in the development of AIDS. He also attempted to make vaccines against HIV, although these efforts, like those of Gallo and numerous other researchers, were not successful. Unfortunately, the college was not able to raise enough money to build the center for AIDS research that it had

Luc Montagnier moved to Queens College (shown here), part of the City University of New York, in 1997. The college promised to build a new AIDS research center, which Montagnier would head. It failed to raise the funds for the project, however, and Montagnier left the college in 2001. (*Queens College*)

In 2002, Luc Montagnier and Robert Gallo announced that they would bury ill feelings and work together to seek an AIDS vaccine. The two men are shown here after addressing the International AIDS Conference in Paris in 2003. *(AP Images)*

promised Montagnier, and he ended his relationship with the institution in 2001. He then returned to Paris to work full time for the World Foundation for AIDS Research and Prevention.

Montagnier and Gallo presented a united front in the fight against AIDS in 2002, calling for more research on the disease, particularly in developing countries. They also announced that they would head a collaborative research program sponsored by Montagnier's Paris foundation, the Program for International Viral Collaboration, which would focus on attempts to develop a vaccine against HIV. "By pooling resources and working in partnership on an international level, we can more quickly move . . . concepts [related to vaccine development] forward at a level that will have a more immediate global impact," a press release from the Institute of Human Virology quoted Montagnier as saying. Gallo added, "We are [now] friends and collaborators and we look forward to this new chapter in which we both strive for new solutions . . . in halting the destructive path of HIV/AIDS."

NOBEL FOR MONTAGNIER

Over the years, Luc Montagnier and Robert Gallo had received many joint awards for their groundbreaking discoveries about HIV and AIDS. These included the Lasker Award for Basic Medical Research (1987), Canada's Gairdner Award (1987), the Japan Prize (1988), the Prince of Asturias Award (2000), and induction into the U.S. National Inventors' Hall of Fame (2004). They did not share, however, in the greatest scientific prize of all. On October 6, 2008, the Nobel committee announced that Luc Montagnier and Françoise Barré-Sinoussi would divide half of that year's Nobel Prize in physiology or medicine for their roles in discovering HIV. The other half of the prize went to Harald zur Hausen (1936–   ), a German virologist who had shown that a virus called papillomavirus causes cancer of the cervix (the neck of the uterus), leading to a vaccine for the disease.

A maximum of three people can share a Nobel Prize, and Robert Gallo's name was conspicuously absent from the Nobel citation. The Nobel Assembly's press release acknowledged that "several groups contributed to the definitive demonstration of HIV as the cause of acquired human immunodeficiency syndrome (AIDS)," but the British newspaper *Guardian* quoted the chair of the Nobel committee, Bertil Fredholm, as saying, "I think it is really well established that the initial discovery of the virus was in the Institut Pasteur." Gallo issued a public statement congratulating Montagnier and Barré-Sinoussi for receiving the honor, but, according to a *New York Times* article about the Nobel Prize, he also admitted to the Associated Press that not being included in the award was a "disappointment." A news article in the October 10, 2008, issue of *Science* quoted Montagnier as saying he was "surprised" that Gallo had not shared in the award and felt "very sorry for Robert Gallo."

In his Nobel lecture, Montagnier outlined what he saw as the best hope for limiting the AIDS epidemic: a vaccine given after infection has occurred, which would help the patient's immune system keep the virus under control. Such a *therapeutic vaccine* would mimic a situation occurring naturally in a few fortunate people who have lived with untreated HIV infection for many years without developing AIDS. "We want to extend what Mother Nature bestows upon a few lucky individuals . . . to a majority of patients," Montagnier told the *Wall Street Journal* shortly after hearing about his Nobel award.

Montagnier explained in his Nobel lecture that the therapeutic vaccine would be part of a treatment program that would begin by treating patients with HAART for three to six months to reduce the amount of virus in their

Luc Montagnier is shown here with the Nobel Prize in physiology or medicine that he received in Stockholm, Sweden, on December 10, 2008. His colleague Françoise Barré-Sinoussi also won a share of the prize, but another colleague, Jean-Claude Chermann, and Montagnier's longtime competitor, Robert Gallo, were not included. *(Olivier Morin/AFP/Getty Images)*

bodies. This would be followed by two weeks of dosing with *antioxidants* (a class of substances that block harmful chemical reactions triggered by the virus) and compounds that stimulate the immune system. The vaccine would then be given in two separate injections, followed by a booster shot at a later time. Montagnier said he hoped that patients would not need to take antiviral drugs after they received the vaccine.

Montagnier stated that he was working to develop a therapeutic vaccine that would sensitize the immune system to the viral proteins that are least likely to change through mutation. (Artificial, harmless proteins would be used in the vaccine.) He admitted that his vaccine had not been successful in preliminary tests, either because patients' immune systems were already too damaged to respond fully to it or because he had not yet found exactly the right proteins to use. Nonetheless, he told the *Chicago Tribune* at about this time, he believed that an effective therapeutic vaccine could be created within five years.

If the therapeutic vaccine proved successful, Montagnier hoped that researchers could make a *preventive vaccine,* using the same virus proteins, to keep infection from occurring. However, he told UNESCO interviewer Jasmina Sopova that he feared that such a vaccine, even if developed, might do more harm than good unless the protection it offered was perfect. Vaccinated people would be likely to overestimate their degree of protection and act in ways that put them at risk of infection, as has happened with groups

Luc Montagnier, shown here at his desk in Paris in 2006, continues to study HIV and AIDS, but in recent years he has also extended the scope of his research to degenerative diseases associated with old age. *(AP Images)*

given experimental vaccines in the past. "Even if we find a preventive vaccine, we must still continue to educate people to behave responsibly to prevent the spread of HIV," he said.

Today, in addition to continuing his work with the World Foundation for AIDS Research and Prevention, Luc Montagnier does research for the similarly named World Foundation for Medical Research and Prevention, an organization he cofounded with Joseph Varon, a physician in Houston, Texas, around the time he won the Nobel Prize. Some of Montagnier's projects concern AIDS, but most of his work focuses on a search for viruses or other microorganisms that may be associated with chronic degenerative diseases that afflict old age, such as Alzheimer's and Parkinson's diseases and cancer. Once he understands the roots of these diseases better, Montagnier hopes he can find ways to prevent them and give people longer, healthier lives. As a *Time* magazine article said of Montagnier in 1992, "The master detective [is] still on the case."

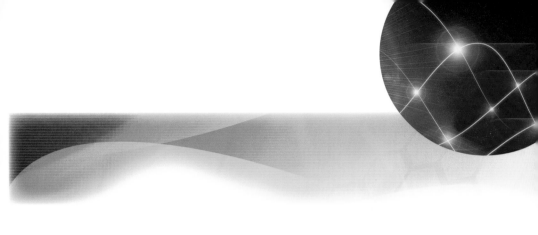

Conclusion

AIDS has killed more than 25 million people since the first cases were identified in 1981, and HIV infection and AIDS still make up a devastating epidemic that touches every part of the world. The Joint United Nations Programme on HIV/AIDS (UNAIDS) reported in 2010 that at the end of 2009 more than 33 million people worldwide were living with HIV. They estimated that in 2009, 1.8 million people died of AIDS and another 2.6 million became infected.

EXTENT OF THE EPIDEMIC

Sub-Saharan Africa, especially southern Africa, is still the area most powerfully affected by the HIV/AIDS epidemic, the UNAIDS report stated. About two-thirds of the people living with AIDS today reside there, even though the continent has only about 10 percent of the world's population. In a few African countries, more than a fifth of the adult population is affected, and AIDS is the single greatest cause of death in Africa as a whole. The high rate of infection has severely damaged the economies of many African countries by killing the young adults who would normally make up most of their workforce, and it has spawned a generation of orphans, many of whom become homeless. (UNAIDS estimates that 16.6 million children worldwide, almost 90 percent of whom live in sub-Saharan Africa, have lost at least one parent to AIDS.) HIV/AIDS is spreading most rapidly in Eastern Europe and

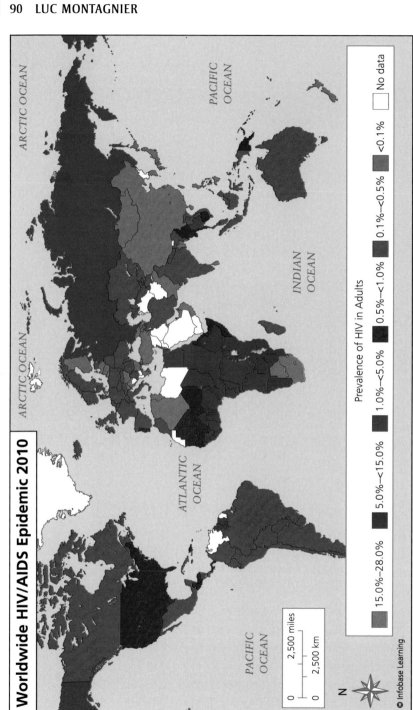

Worldwide HIV/AIDS Epidemic 2010

Prevalence of HIV in Adults

15.0%–28.0%   5.0%–<15.0%   1.0%–<5.0%   0.5%–<1.0%   0.1%–<0.5%   <0.1%   No data

© Infobase Learning

Central Asia, where the number of people with HIV increased from 760,000 in 2001 to 1.4 million in 2009. Social disruption in the countries of the former Soviet Union, especially the Russian Federation, Ukraine, and the Baltic states (Estonia, Latvia, and Lithuania), has encouraged the infection, which occurs there mostly among intravenous drug users.

Most (96 percent) of HIV/AIDS cases today are in the developing world, but the disease has by no means vanished from industrialized countries. UNAIDS estimated that about 2.3 million people are living with HIV in North America and western and central Europe—an increase of 30 percent since 2001. The CDC stated that about 1.1 million people were currently living with HIV in the United States, and 53,600 new infections were occurring yearly. The highest rate of new infection (52 percent) was in African Americans. New, extremely accurate tests have removed the HIV threat from the U.S. blood supply, and drug treatment has also greatly reduced transmission from infected mothers to their children. Risky behavior continues to expose new people to the virus, however. Many U.S. citizens with HIV have access to the antiretroviral medications needed to control the infection, either through health insurance or through programs such as the Ryan White CARE Act, but a substantial number still do not.

HIV infection spreads in the same ways it always has, primarily through shared intravenous drug equipment and unprotected sex, especially sex with multiple partners. Men and women are now infected in about equal numbers, with women slightly in the lead (52 percent of people living with HIV/AIDS). Because most HIV transmission involves behaviors that can be changed, education remains the most important way of preventing the disease. The facts that the percentage of people infected worldwide seems to have leveled off and the number of new infections has fallen by 19 percent between 1999 and 2009 suggest that education and other prevention efforts have made significant headway. In the long term, however, stopping the epidemic may prove impossible unless the social conditions that foster the disease, such as the poverty and disruption that pushes people toward drug use and the powerlessness that makes many women sexually vulnerable, are changed.

(*opposite page*) HIV/AIDS is still a major cause of death in many parts of the world. Africa remains the continent most devastated by the disease, with southern Africa especially hard hit. HIV/AIDS has also spread widely in eastern Europe and parts of Asia.

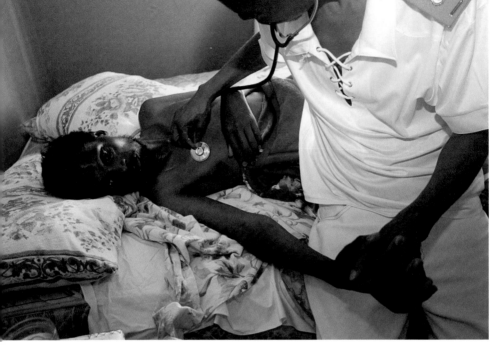

Although effective treatments for HIV/AIDS now exist, many infected people in the developing world do not have access to them. Here, a physician treats a 30-year-old man with AIDS in Siteki, eastern Swaziland, in 2004. *(Alexander Joe/AFP/Getty Images)*

Combinations of antiretroviral drugs, if given soon enough and taken consistently, can keep most HIV infections under control and prevent their progressing to full-blown AIDS. AZT and other drugs can stop the virus from spreading from infected mothers to their babies, and opportunistic infections that arise in the wake of AIDS can also be treated. Since the year 2000, drug companies have made antiviral medications available at cost to developing countries and have allowed cheaper, generic versions of the drugs to be made for sale there. Partly as a result, the number of people in the developing world receiving treatment has increased by 13 times between 2004 and 2009. An additional 1.2 million people received antiretroviral drugs in 2009 alone.

In spite of these advances, only about a third of the world's HIV-infected people have access to anti-HIV drugs. Part of the problem is that developing countries often do not have the doctors and other medical personnel needed to administer and monitor the treatments. In addition, people there are often unwilling to be tested or treated for HIV because prejudice against persons with HIV/AIDS is still strong in many places. Those who admit to having the infection risk being shunned or sometimes physically attacked by acquaintances or even members of their own families.

HOPE FOR THE FUTURE

Funding to combat the HIV/AIDS epidemic has increased greatly in the 2000s. Most of the money has come from governments of developed countries such as the United States; the U.S. government, in fact, is the largest single donor to worldwide AIDS relief, accounting for 58 percent of all government-donated money for AIDS relief and 27 percent of AIDS funding from all sources. The governments of countries strongly affected by the epidemic, international organizations such as UNAIDS and Luc Montagnier's World Foundation for AIDS Research and Prevention, and private charities such as the Bill and Melinda Gates Foundation (which had spent more than $2.3 billion on AIDS relief by 2009) have also contributed. UNAIDS reports, however, that because of hard economic times worldwide, the total amount of money that governments across the globe donated to fight the AIDS epidemic in 2009 was slightly less than in 2008. "The gap between investment needs and resource availability is widening," the agency says. It states that total available funding in 2010 was $10 billion less than the needed amount.

UNAIDS sounds an overall note of hope in its 2010 report. For example, it points out that the number of people living with HIV has risen by 27 percent between 1999 and 2009 because increased access to antiviral drugs has made the number of deaths from AIDS-related causes drop substantially. For example, 20 percent fewer people in sub-Saharan Africa died of AIDS in 2009 than in 2004, when access to such drugs began to be dramatically expanded. The incidence of new infections has also dropped by more than 25 percent in 33 countries, including 22 in sub-Saharan Africa.

Nonetheless, "the[se] gains are real but still fragile," the report emphasizes.

> UNAIDS' vision of zero discrimination, zero new infections and zero AIDS-related deaths poses a challenge. But it is not a hopeless challenge. The vision of eliminating the toll that HIV imposes on human life can be made real using the knowledge and resources available today.

Luc Montagnier and thousands of other scientists worldwide continue to seek a vaccine or a cure for AIDS, but this remains a daunting task. New antiviral drugs continue to appear, replacing those to which strains of the virus have developed resistance, but none is likely to provide a final answer to the epidemic. Part of the problem is that the virus can hide for years in inactive CD4 cells and other cell types, waiting to emerge once more if infected people stop taking antiviral drugs. UNAIDS places much of its hope in its Treatment 2.0 program, which aims to simplify the way treatment is provided and scale up access to existing drugs rather than search for new medications. The agency's 2010 report claims that the program potentially could avert 10 million deaths by 2025 and could reduce new infections by up to 1 million annually.

HIV's ability to mutate rapidly makes development of a vaccine equally challenging. According to the International AIDS Vaccine Initiative's database, 22 trials of preventive AIDS vaccines were taking place around the world in 2010, but most of the vaccines were in the earliest stages of human testing. The largest trial to date, involving more than 16,000 volunteers in Thailand, produced optimistic results in September 2009, when spokespeople from the trial's sponsors, the U.S. Army and the National Institute of Allergy and Infectious Diseases, announced that a combination of two vaccines had cut the risk of infection by more than 31 percent. This is a better success rate than any other vaccine (including these same two vaccines when tested separately) has achieved. Nonetheless, the study's authors called the combination's effects merely "modest," and many researchers believe that this will be true of future vaccines as well. Luc Montagnier and others have pointed out the danger that people who receive a vaccine might believe their protection to be greater than it really is and therefore will indulge in behaviors that expose them to the virus, possibly becoming infected as a result.

Many AIDS charities believe that control of the global HIV/AIDS epidemic, if it occurs, will come through more effective prevention efforts and making sure that all who need them receive existing treatments rather than through new scientific breakthroughs. Luc Montagnier, however, refuses to give up hope. "We are not dead in AIDS research," Montagnier told *Internal Medicine News* reporter Lorinda Bullock in June 2009. "There are still new discoveries to be made."

Chronology

1911
Peyton Rous shows that a virus can cause cancer in chickens

August 18, 1932
Luc Montagnier is born in Chabris, France

1949
Montagnier enters University of Poitiers

early 1950s
Montagnier does research on how water plants react to sunlight

1953
Montagnier earns bachelor's degree in natural science from University of Poitiers; James Watson and Francis Crick discover the structure of the DNA molecule

1955
Montagnier earns licentiate in science from University of Paris; becomes assistant in cell biology at the Institut Curie and teaches at the Sorbonne

1959
First known case of what is later identified as AIDS occurs in the Belgian Congo

1960
Montagnier earns doctorate in medicine from the University of Paris; begins doing postdoctoral research in England

1961
Montagnier marries Dorothea Ackerman

1963
Montagnier shows that the RNA of a virus becomes a double-stranded helix when the virus reproduces; moves to University of Glasgow in Scotland

1964

Montagnier develops a way to grow cancer cells in agar; returns to France and the Institut Curie

1965

Montagnier shows that viruses' ability to infect cells and reproduce can be separated from their ability to cause cancer

1965–1972

Montagnier directs laboratory at Institut Curie in Orsay

1970

Howard Temin and David Baltimore discover reverse transcriptase

1972

Montagnier moves to Institut Pasteur and becomes head of new viral oncology unit

1973

Two California scientists invent genetic engineering

1974

Scientists in the United States set up safety standards for genetic engineering research

early 1970s

Montagnier studies interferon

1976

Michael Bishop and Harold Varmus show that cancer-causing genes are altered forms of normal cell genes rather than coming from viruses

1977

Montagnier's laboratory uses anti-interferon serum in attempts to find viruses that cause human cancer

late 1970s

Occasional cases of AIDS occur but are not recognized

1979

Robert Gallo discovers HTLV-1, the first virus shown to cause cancer in humans; Gallo and Montagnier begin collaboration

June 5, 1981

Michael Gottlieb's article about unusual cases of pneumonia in homosexual men is published in *Morbidity and Mortality Weekly Report (MMWR)*; this is the first description in medical literature of the disease later known as AIDS

July 3, 1981
Alvin Friedman-Kien reports cases of gay men developing Kaposi's sarcoma, a cancer later associated with AIDS

late 1981
Willy Rozenbaum and other physicians in Paris begin seeing and tracking cases of illness similar to those reported in *MMWR;* James Curran of the Centers for Disease Control (CDC) tries to interest National Institutes of Health (NIH) scientists in the new disease; the disease is detected in intravenous drug users

December 1981
Answers to a CDC questionnaire suggest that the disease spreads through sexual activity

mid-1982
The disease is reported in hemophiliacs who receive multiple blood transfusions, suggesting that the disease agent has infected the U.S. blood supply; Robert Gallo decides to search for a virus that may cause the disease

late 1982
The illness is named AIDS (acquired immunodeficiency syndrome)

December 1982
AIDS is reported in babies, most of whom appear to have caught it from their mothers; Luc Montagnier begins looking for a possible AIDS virus

January 3, 1983
Montagnier begins culturing lymph node tissue from Frédéric Brugière

late January 1983
The Brugière culture shows reverse transcriptase activity, but the cells begin to die; Montagnier rescues the culture by adding fresh T cells

February 4, 1983
Charles Dauguet makes electron microscope photographs of a virus in the culture

late February 1983
Montagnier's group finds that antibodies to HTLV-1 do not react with their virus

spring 1983
Robert Gallo's laboratory finds signs of retrovirus infection in cell cultures from AIDS patients

April 1983
Montagnier submits a paper about his virus to *Science;* Mathilde Krim founds the first private AIDS charity

May 20, 1983
Montagnier's paper appears in *Science* along with two papers by Gallo and two by Myron Essex

June 1983
Montagnier's group names their virus LAV (lymphadenopathy-associated virus)

July 1983
Montagnier brings samples of LAV to Gallo and speaks to the National Cancer Institute's task force on AIDS

August 1983
Montagnier team completes ELISA blood test for antibodies to LAV

September 14–15, 1983
Montagnier presents his research at Cold Spring Harbor meeting

mid-September 1983
Institut Pasteur applies for U.S. patent on its AIDS blood test

late September 1983
Barré-Sinoussi brings more samples of LAV to Gallo

fall 1983
Montagnier group grows LAV in a B-cell line; Mikulas Popovic of Gallo's laboratory grows virus from pooled cultures in a T-cell line

February 1984
Jean-Claude Chermann presents Montagnier laboratory's work at meeting in Park City, Utah

early 1984
Montagnier's and Gallo's ELISA tests obtain excellent results with blood samples from the CDC

March 1984
Gallo names his candidate virus HTLV-3

April 23, 1984
NIH applies for patent on Gallo laboratory's blood test; Margaret Heckler announces in press conference that Gallo has discovered the cause of AIDS

May 4, 1984
Four papers from Gallo's laboratory appear in *Science,* providing evidence that they have found the virus that causes AIDS

mid-May 1984
A researcher from Gallo's laboratory brings sample of HTLV-3 to Montagnier's laboratory for comparison with LAV

July 1984
Gallo tells Montagnier that restriction maps of HTLV-3 and LAV are very similar and suggests that HTLV-3 must have contaminated the LAV cultures; Montagnier strongly rejects this idea

mid-1984
Abbott Laboratories, Genetic Systems, and other companies begin developing commercial forms of the Gallo and Montagnier blood tests

fall 1984
Montagnier's laboratory discovers a second AIDS virus

November 1984
Gallo and Montagnier laboratories determine the sequence of bases in their viruses' genomes

January 1985
Papers from the two laboratories show that the base sequences of HTLV-3 and LAV are almost identical

early 1985
Sequencing shows that some genes of the AIDS virus mutate much more often than those of other viruses

March 1985
The U.S. Food and Drug Administration (FDA) gives Abbott Laboratories permission to sell a blood test kit based on Gallo's virus

May 1985
U.S. Patent and Trademark Office awards patent for Gallo laboratory's blood test

December 12, 1985
Institut Pasteur sues U.S. government, asking for a share of royalties from the blood test

February 1986
FDA gives Genetic Systems permission to sell blood test kit based on Montagnier's virus

April 18, 1986
Gallo admits in *Science* that a photograph in one of the May 1984 papers that was labeled as being HTLV-3 actually showed LAV

May 1986
An international committee names the AIDS virus HIV (human immuno-deficiency virus); patent office decision supports Institut Pasteur

September 11, 1986
After success in a large-scale test on human patients, azidothymidine (AZT) begins to be sold as the first widely accepted treatment for AIDS

March 31, 1987
U.S. president Ronald Reagan and French premier Jacques Chirac ratify an international agreement that divides credit and patent royalties evenly between NIH and the Institut Pasteur

1987
Montagnier and Gallo share Gairdner Award and Lasker Award; Institut Pasteur gives Montagnier a whole floor in the institute's new retrovirology building

1988
Montagnier and Gallo share the Japan Prize

November 19, 1989
In a long article in the *Chicago Tribune,* reporter John Crewdson accuses Gallo of possibly having misappropriated Montagnier's virus

January 1990
NIH's Office of Scientific Integrity begins investigating Gallo's role in the discovery of HIV

1990
Montagnier claims that mycoplasma may be a cofactor in causing AIDS

1991
Montagnier's laboratory shows that HIV damages the immune system by triggering a cell suicide program and by stressing the system

February 28, 1991
Gallo states in *Nature* that the base sequence of the virus that Montagnier brought to his laboratory in July 1983 is not the same as the sequence of HTLV-3B or LAV

May 1991

Montagnier's laboratory discovers that a virus from Christophe Lailier (LAV-Lai) had contaminated the laboratory's other virus cultures in late summer 1983; it was unknowingly brought to Gallo's laboratory and contaminated that laboratory's cultures as well

May 30, 1991

Gallo admits that HTLV-3B is a French virus

December 1992

Office of Research Integrity (ORI) finds Mika Popovic and Robert Gallo guilty of scientific misconduct because of errors in Popovic's May 1984 *Science* paper

November 1993

Research Integrity Adjudications Panel reverses ORI verdict against Popovic; ORI then drops charges against Gallo

1993

Large British-French test of AZT shows that the drug slows AIDS progress only temporarily; Luc Montagnier and Federico Mayor establish the World Foundation for AIDS Research and Prevention

July 11, 1994

Because of the discovery that the virus used in the AIDS blood tests originated in France, the Board of the French and American AIDS Foundation awards the Institut Pasteur a greater share of the patent royalties for the tests than it had received before

1996–1997

A new type of drug (protease inhibitors) and a new form of combination drug therapy substantially reduce the number of deaths from AIDS in developed countries

1997

Montagnier retires from Institut Pasteur and joins Queens College in New York City

1999

Researchers find a simian immunodeficiency virus that infects chimpanzees; it may be the "missing link" between monkey viruses and HIV

2000

Montagnier and Gallo share Prince of Asturias Award; drug companies agree to make antiretroviral drugs available to developing countries at cost

2001

Montagnier leaves Queens College and returns to Paris

2002

Montagnier and Gallo establish a collaborative research program to develop an AIDS vaccine

2003

Researchers propose that the chimpanzee virus that probably became HIV may have arisen when two kinds of monkey virus infected chimpanzees at the same time and combined their genetic material

2004

Montagnier and Gallo are inducted into the U.S. National Inventors' Hall of Fame

2008

Montagnier and Joseph Varon establish World Foundation for Medical Research and Prevention

October 6, 2008

Montagnier and Barré-Sinoussi win half of the 2008 Nobel Prize in physiology or medicine; Gallo does not share the award

September 2009

A combination of two AIDS vaccines produces promising results in a large human trial in Thailand

2010

Joint United Nations Programme on HIV/AIDS (UNAIDS) issues new report claiming "real but still fragile" gains against the global AIDS epidemic, including overall declines in both new infections and AIDS-related deaths and an increase in the number of people receiving antiviral drugs.

Glossary

agar a jellylike material made from seaweed, used as a nutrient substance in laboratory cultures of bacteria and, sometimes, cells.

AIDS (acquired immunodeficiency syndrome) name given in late 1982 to a new disease marked by destruction of CD4 lymphocytes and presence of opportunistic infections; the disease was later shown to be caused by HIV. *See also* **HIV**.

amino acids small molecules of which proteins are composed.

antibodies substances made by the immune system that attach to proteins that do not belong to the body and mark them for destruction; a particular type of antibody fits only one kind of protein.

antioxidants substances that prevent certain types of chemical reactions that harm cells.

apoptosis a genetic program that tells a cell to self-destruct.

azidothymidine (AZT; also called zidovudine) a drug that keeps HIV from reproducing by blocking the action of reverse transcriptase; it was the first approved treatment for AIDS.

bases four types of small molecules of which DNA and RNA are made.

biopsy a small piece of tissue removed from the body so that doctors can examine it to find out what illness a person has.

CD4 lymphocyte one of several types of T cell made by the immune system; HIV specifically infects and destroys this kind of cell. *See also* **helper T cell**.

cell line a group of cells, all descendants of a single cell, that reproduces endlessly in laboratory culture.

clone an exact genetic duplicate of another cell or organism; to make such a duplicate.

cofactor an agent that does not cause a disease but must be present in order for the disease to occur.

contagious disease a disease that can be spread directly from one living thing to another. *Compare* **infectious disease**.

culture a colony of cells or microorganisms maintained in a laboratory.

cytoplasm a jellylike substance that makes up the main body of a cell.

deoxyribonucleic acid (DNA) a complex biochemical that carries genetic information in most types of organism. *See also* **ribonucleic acid (RNA)**.

double-blind test a test of a medical treatment in which neither patients nor their doctors know whether a particular patient is receiving the drug or an inactive treatment (placebo).

ELISA (enzyme-linked immunosorbent assay) test a test that uses proteins from viruses or other microorganisms, attached to marker chemicals, to show whether antibodies to those microorganisms are present in a sample of blood.

enzyme one of a number of proteins that speed up biochemical reactions or allow the reactions to occur.

epidemic a major outbreak of infectious disease, in which large numbers of people or animals become ill with the same disease at approximately the same time and place. *See also* **infectious disease**.

Factor VIII a substance in blood that allows the blood to clot; it is extracted from blood and given to people with hemophilia, whose bodies cannot make it.

false negative a test result that shows that antibodies, microorganisms or the like are not present in a sample when in fact they are there. *Compare* **false positive**.

false positive a test result that shows that antibodies, microorganisms or the like are present in a sample when in fact the sample does not contain them. *Compare* **false negative**.

feline leukemia virus (FeLV) a retrovirus that can cause either blood cell cancer or immune system suppression in cats.

gene a stretch of DNA that carries the coded information for a single function, such as making a protein or controlling another gene.

genetic engineering the act of artificially recombining or altering genes, for instance by inserting a gene from one species of organism into the genome of another.

genome an organism's complete collection of genes.

HAART (highly active antiretroviral therapy) a treatment for HIV/AIDS developed in the mid-1990s, in which several (usually three) different classes of drugs are combined to minimize the chances that HIV will develop resistance to the treatment.

helix   a coiled shape, like a spring or a corkscrew; the molecules of nucleic acids and many proteins have this shape.

helper T cell   a type of immune system cell, also called a CD4 lymphocyte, which directs the activities of most other cells in the system. *See also* **CD4 lymphocyte**.

hemophilia   an inherited disease whose sufferers (hemophiliacs) cannot make a protein needed for blood clotting (Factor VIII); as a result, they can bleed to death from even a slight injury if not treated.

HIV (human immunodeficiency virus)   the retrovirus that almost all scientists believe to be the cause of AIDS. *See also* **AIDS**.

HTLV-1 (human T-cell leukemia virus 1)   a retrovirus, discovered by Robert Gallo in 1979, that causes a rare form of human leukemia.

HTLV-3   Robert Gallo's name for the retrovirus later known as HIV.

HTLV-3B   the specific strain of HTLV-3 that Gallo's laboratory used in developing its blood test for the virus; it was later shown to be identical to one strain of LAV. *See also* **HIV**; **LAV**.

immune system   the body's defense system, a collection of cells and chemicals that attack and destroy substances foreign to the body.

infectious disease   a disease caused by a microorganism; many infectious diseases, but not all, are contagious. *Compare* **contagious disease**.

interferon   a substance made by virus-infected cells to alert the immune system to the infection.

interleukin-2   a substance that helps T cells survive in culture.

intravenous drugs   drugs taken by injection into the bloodstream; heroin is an example.

Kaposi's sarcoma   a type of skin cancer, formerly rare but now often associated with AIDS.

LAV (lymphadenopathy-associated virus)   Luc Montagnier's name for the virus later known as HIV. *See also* **HIV**; **HTLV-3**.

lentivirus ("slow virus")   a family of retroviruses causing illnesses that produce no symptoms for a considerable length of time after infection.

leukemia   a cancer of white blood cells (immune system cells).

lymph   a clear fluid, part of the immune system, that circulates in a separate system of vessels called the lymph system.

lymphadenopathy   an abnormal medical condition in which the lymph glands are swollen; it can be a forerunner of AIDS.

lymph gland   one of a number of nodes of tissue in various parts of the body, such as under the arms, where immune system cells gather.

lymphocyte   one of several types of immune system cell carried in lymph and blood.

lymph system   a system of glands and vessels that carry lymph and certain types of immune system cells (lymphocytes).

molecular biology   the branch of science that investigates biological processes by studying the structure and function of the complex molecules in the bodies of living things.

mutate   change; said of a gene in which the sequence of bases has become altered.

mycoplasma   a type of small bacterium that sometimes causes disease; Luc Montagnier thinks some kinds of mycoplasma may be cofactors in AIDS.

nucleus   the central body of a cell, containing its main genetic material.

oncogene   a gene that causes cancer; oncogenes have been shown to be mutated forms of normal genes involved in cell reproduction and growth.

opportunistic infection   an infection that the immune system normally can control but that causes disease if the immune system is weakened.

PCR (polymerase chain reaction)   a technique that can multiply tiny amounts of DNA, allowing the DNA to be studied more easily.

placebo   a fake medical treatment that contains no active ingredients; it is sometimes given as part of a test of a new medication, for comparison purposes. *See also* **double-blind test**.

Pneumocystis carinii   a microscopic parasite that is normally harmless to humans but can cause pneumonia in people whose immune systems are weakened.

pneumonia   a lung disease; it can be caused by a variety of bacteria and other microorganisms.

preventive vaccine   a vaccine given to uninfected people to prevent infection by a particular type of microorganism. *Compare* **therapeutic vaccine**.

protease inhibitor   a class of drugs first used against HIV in the mid-1990s; it blocks viral enzymes called proteases.

protein   one of a large group of biochemicals that does most of the work in cells.

provirus   a segment of cellular DNA that matches part of the genetic sequence of a virus.

restriction enzyme   one of a group of enzymes that bacteria make to protect themselves against viruses by cutting the strands of the viruses' nucleic acid.

restriction map   a list of the fragments made by treating a sample of nucleic acid with restriction enzymes.

retrovirus ("backwards virus")   a virus that has RNA as its genetic material and uses reverse transcriptase to copy that RNA into DNA, which it then inserts into the genomes of the cells it infects.

reverse transcriptase   an enzyme by which retroviruses copy their RNA into DNA that can be inserted into a cell's genome; only retroviruses make this enzyme, so its presence in a cell is evidence that the cell is infected by a retrovirus.

ribonucleic acid (RNA)   a nucleic acid, related to DNA but containing one different kind of base; it is the genetic material of some kinds of viruses and also plays an important role in making proteins and some other biochemical activities in cells. *Compare* **deoxyribonucleic acid.**

Rous sarcoma virus   the first kind of virus shown to cause cancer in animals; it produces a cancer in chickens.

sequencing   the act of determining the exact sequence (order) of bases in a DNA molecule.

serum   the clear (cell-free) part of the blood, which contains antibodies. *See also* **antibodies.**

side effects   unwanted effects of a medical treatment.

simian immunodeficiency virus (SIV)   one of a number of retroviruses that infect different kinds of monkeys, sometimes causing immune system damage; one of these is thought to have been the ancestor of HIV.

slim   African name for AIDS.

symptoms   signs of illness.

syndrome   a group of symptoms that usually occur together.

T cells   immune system cells that are made in the thymus, a gland in the neck.

therapeutic vaccine   a vaccine given after infection to strengthen the immune system and help it keep the infection under control. *Compare* **preventive vaccine.**

tuberculosis   a serious disease caused by a bacterium that usually affects the lungs.

virology   the study of viruses.

virus   an extremely small microorganism that can reproduce only inside living cells.

white cells   cells of the immune system, found in the blood and lymph.

Further Resources

Books

Connor, Steve, and Sharon Kingman. *The Search for the Virus*. New York: Viking Penguin, 1988.

Overview of the early years of the HIV/AIDS epidemic and the search for the virus that causes the disease.

Crewdson, John. *Science Fictions: A Scientific Mystery, a Massive Cover-up, and the Dark Legacy of Robert Gallo*. Boston: Little, Brown, 2002.

Presents a detailed description of Gallo's role in the discovery of HIV, including his interactions with Luc Montagnier, and of the investigation into Gallo's conduct in the early 1990s. Crewdson, an investigative reporter for the Chicago Tribune, *is strongly critical of Gallo. Sources for the many reference citations in the book can be found at http://www.sciencefictions.net/citations.php.*

Engel, Jonathan. *The Epidemic: A Global History of AIDS*. New York: HarperCollins/Smithsonian Books, 2006.

Focuses on the spread of the AIDS epidemic worldwide and people's reactions to it, through the mid-2000s.

Gallo, Robert. *Virus Hunting: AIDS, Cancer, and the Human Retrovirus: A Story of Scientific Discovery*. New York: HarperCollins/New Republic/Basic Books, 1991.

Gallo's autobiography, focusing on his laboratory's role in the discovery of HTLV-1, the first virus shown to cause cancer in humans, and HIV. The book includes some information about Gallo's relationship with Montagnier. Its narrative ends around 1987, but Gallo includes an afterword in which he answers some of John Crewdson's accusations.

Kulstad, Ruth, ed. *AIDS: Papers from* Science, *1982–1985*. Washington, D.C.: American Association for the Advancement of Science, 1986.

This collection from the American journal Science *presents a number of key papers from the earliest years of the AIDS epidemic, including the Montag-*

nier laboratory's first published description of the virus later called HIV. Papers from Robert Gallo's laboratory and news articles about the development of the epidemic are also included.

Lapierre, Dominique. *Beyond Love.* Translated by Kathryn Spink. New York: Time Warner, 1991.

Lapierre describes the development of the AIDS epidemic through 1987 by means of several alternating narratives, one of which is a detailed description of the Montagnier and Gallo laboratories' search for the virus that causes the disease. Although Lapierre writes in a novelistic style, his material is factual, based on interviews.

Montagnier, Luc. *Virus: The Co-Discoverer of HIV Tracks Its Rampage and Charts the Future.* Translated by Stephen Sartarelli. New York: Norton, 1994.

Part of this book is Montagnier's autobiography, providing some information about his early life and career but concentrating on his activities during the search for the AIDS virus (1982–87). The rest is a discussion, now dated for the most part, about the virus, the AIDS epidemic, and hopes for controlling it.

"Montagnier, Luc." In *Current Biography Yearbook 1988.* New York: H. W. Wilson, 1988.

Article summarizes Montagnier's career through 1988, including his pioneering research on the virus that causes AIDS and his disputes with Robert Gallo.

Shilts, Randy. *And the Band Played On: Politics, People, and the AIDS Epidemic.* New York: St. Martin's Press, 1987.

This account of the early years of the AIDS epidemic (to 1987), by a reporter who later died of the disease, focuses on reactions to the epidemic among health professionals and the gay (male homosexual) community in San Francisco but also includes information on the search for the AIDS agent by the Gallo and Montagnier laboratories and the Centers for Disease Control (CDC).

Internet Resources

"AIDS & HIV Around the World." AVERT.org. Available online. URL: http://www.avert.org/aroundworld.htm. Accessed May 11, 2011.

Summary of the AIDS epidemic in different parts of the world as of 2009, based on the 2010 UNAIDS/WHO report.

"AIDS and HIV Information from AVERT.org." AVERT.org. Available online. URL: http://www.avert.org. Accessed May 11, 2011.

Web site of this British-based international AIDS charity provides a wealth of information about the HIV/AIDS epidemic, including detailed year-by-year histories, scientific information, articles about HIV/AIDS in different regions and groups, photos, personal stories, and games and quizzes.

"AIDS Timeline." AVERT.org. Last updated August 21, 2009. Available online. URL: http://www.avert.org/aids-timeline.htm. Accessed May 11, 2011.

Lists major events related to the spread of AIDS, science and prevention, national action, treatment, and global action over a time period beginning before the 1970s and ending in 2010.

Barré-Sinoussi, Françoise. "HIV: A Discovery Opening the Road to Novel Scientific Knowledge and Global Health Improvement." Nobelprize.org. December 7, 2008. Available online. URL: http://nobelprize.org/nobel_prizes/medicine/laureates/2008/barre-sinoussi-lecture.html. Accessed May 11, 2011.

Web page on the Nobel Prize site links to video and PDF versions of Barré-Sinoussi's Nobel Prize lecture, which describes the events surrounding the discovery of HIV and the state of the HIV/AIDS epidemic today. Barré-Sinoussi emphasizes that HIV research provides benefits reaching beyond the epidemic, such as a better understanding of the immune system's response to infection.

de Boer, Bonita, and Gemma Spink. "HIV and AIDS in America." AVERT.org. Last updated November 4, 2009. Available online. URL: http://www.avert.org/america.htm. Accessed May 11, 2011.

Describes HIV/AIDS in the United States today (most recent statistics 2011), including groups most affected and the current state of HIV/AIDS prevention, treatment, care, and funding.

"The Discovery of the AIDS Virus in 1983." Institut Pasteur. Available online. URL: http://www.pasteur.fr/ip/easysite/go/03b-000027-00i/the-discovery-of-the-aids-virus-in-1983. Accessed May 11, 2011.

This press release presents the Pasteur Institute's version of the events involved in the discovery of HIV.

"The Evidence That HIV Causes AIDS." National Institute of Allergy and Infectious Diseases. Available online. URL: http://www.niaid.nih.gov/topics/hivaids/understanding/howhivcausesaids/pages/hivcausesaids.aspx. Accessed May 11, 2011.

This document from NIAID, part of the National Institutes of Health, provides extensive evidence that HIV causes AIDS and answers the questions that Peter Duesberg and other "AIDS denialists" have raised.

"The Global HIV/AIDS Epidemic." The Henry J. Kaiser Family Foundation. November 2009. Available online. URL: http://www.kff.org/hivaids/upload/3030-14.pdf. Accessed May 11, 2011.

This fact sheet summarizes the most recent available statistics on the worldwide AIDS epidemic. Most are figures for 2007, from a 2008 report by the Joint United Nations Programme on HIV/AIDS (UNAIDS) and the World Health Organization (WHO).

"Global Report: UNAIDS Report on the Global AIDS Epidemic 2010." UNAIDS (Joint United Nations Programme on HIV/AIDS). 2010. Available online. URL: http://www.unaids.org/globalreport/documents/20101123_GlobalReport_full_en.pdf. Accessed May 11, 2011.

The latest edition of this authoritative report on the worldwide AIDS epidemic features statistics from 2009, including numerous charts and graphs. It covers current prevalence of AIDS, including new infections and deaths; prevention; treatment; the relationship between AIDS and human rights/gender equality; and financing of efforts to combat the epidemic.

"A Historical Summary of Dr. Robert Gallo." Institute of Human Virology. Available online. URL: http://www.ihv.org/about/Robert-Gallo.html. Accessed May 11, 2011.

This account of Gallo's career, published by the institution he heads, stresses his many achievements.

"In Their Own Words . . . NIH Researchers Recall the Early Years of AIDS." National Institutes of Health. Available online. URL: http://history.nih.gov/NIHInOwnWords. Accessed May 11, 2011.

In this collection of oral history interviews made in the early 1990s, Robert Gallo and other NIH scientists recall their reactions to the burgeoning AIDS epidemic in the 1980s. In addition to transcripts of the interviews, the site includes a timeline for the period, a document archive, and an image archive.

Kanabus, Annabel, Sarah Allen, and Bonita de Boer. "The Origin of AIDS and HIV and the First Cases of AIDS." AVERT.org. Available online. URL: http://www.avert.org/origin-aids-hiv.htm. Accessed on May 11, 2011.

Explains the theory, currently accepted by most AIDS researchers, that HIV developed from a chimpanzee virus that in turn evolved from retroviruses that infect African monkeys. The paper also considers how the virus might have begin to infect to humans and how, why, where, and when AIDS became an epidemic. It discusses several alternate theories about the origin of AIDS as well.

"Luc Montagnier Biography (1932–   )." Faqs.org. Last updated February 11, 2004. Available online. URL: http://www.faqs.org/health/bios/61/Luc-Montagnier.html. Accessed May 11, 2011.

Brief summary of Montagnier's life through the mid-1990s, with one 2004 update.

Montagnier, Luc. "Twenty-Five Years After HIV Discovery: Prospects for Cure and Vaccine." Nobelprize.org. December 7, 2008. Available online. URL: http://nobelprize.org/nobel_prizes/medicine/laureates/2008/montagnier-lecture.html. Accessed May 11, 2011.

This page provides links to Montagnier's Nobel lecture in video and printed (PDF) form. In his lecture, Montagnier gives a brief history of the AIDS epidemic and his successful search for the virus that causes the disease. He also considers prospects for future control of the epidemic.

Noble, Rob. "A Cure for AIDS." AVERT.org. Last updated August 21, 2009. Available online. URL: http://www.avert.org/cure-for-aids.htm. Accessed May 11, 2011.

Explains why finding a cure for AIDS has been so difficult, what the prospects are, how to spot fake AIDS cures, and why such cures are so dangerous.

———. "HIV Is the Cause of AIDS." AVERT.org. Available online. URL: http://www.avert.org/hiv-causes-aids.htm. Accessed December 26, 2010.

Provides extensive evidence to answer AIDS denialists' claims that HIV does not really cause AIDS.

———. "Introduction to the AIDS Epidemic." AVERT.org. Last updated October 28, 2009. Available online. URL: http://www.avert.org/aids-hiv.htm. Accessed May 11, 2011.

Brief overview of the present worldwide HIV/AIDS epidemic.

———, and Gemma Spink. "AIDS Vaccine." AVERT.org. Last updated October 23, 2009. Available online. URL: http://www.avert.org/aids-vaccine.htm. Accessed May 11, 2011.

Explains why developing a vaccine against HIV/AIDS is so difficult and surveys past and present vaccine trials.

"Virusmyth: A Rethinking AIDS Website." Virusmyth.com. Available online. URL: http://www.virusmyth.com. Accessed May 11, 2011.

This AIDS denialist Web site presents reasons for believing that HIV does not cause AIDS.

"World Foundation for AIDS Research and Prevention." UNESCO. Available online. URL: http://erc.unesco.org/ong/en/Directory/ONG_Desc. asp?mode=gn&code=1459. Accessed May 11, 2011.

Brief description of the international AIDS research organization that Luc Montagnier founded in 1993 under the auspices of UNESCO (United Nations Education, Scientific, and Cultural Organization).

Periodicals

Altman, Lawrence K. "Discoverers of AIDS and Cancer Viruses Win Nobel." *New York Times,* October 7, 2008, p. A8.

Article describes the achievements of Luc Montagnier, Françoise Barré-Sinoussi, and Harald zur Hausen, winners of the 2008 Nobel Prize in physiology or medicine, and explains why Robert Gallo was not included in the award.

Arenson, Karen W. "College Returns $3 Million Gift for AIDS Lab." *New York Times,* March 17, 2001.

Explains that Queens College, part of the City University of New York, has been unable to raise sufficient funds to build the AIDS research center that it had promised Luc Montagnier when he joined the Queens College faculty in 1997.

Barré-Sinoussi, F., et al. "Isolation of a T-lymphotropic Retrovirus from a Patient at Risk for Acquired Immune Deficiency Syndrome (AIDS)." *Science* 220 (May 20, 1983): 868–871.

This is the Montagnier laboratory's first paper describing their isolation of the retrovirus that was later shown to cause AIDS.

Bullock, Lorinda. "Twenty-Five Years Later, HIV/AIDS Still an Epidemic." *Internal Medicine News* 42 (June 1, 2009): 14.

Brief news update on the global HIV/AIDS epidemic includes comments from Luc Montagnier and Robert Gallo.

Cohen, Jon. "The Duesberg Phenomenon." *Science* 266 (December 9, 1994): 1,642–1,644.

This news article describes and refutes the views of University of California, Berkeley, virologist Peter Duesberg and his supporters, who deny that HIV causes AIDS.

———. "Longtime Rivalry Ends in Collaboration." *Science* 295 (February 22, 2002): 1,441–1,442.

News article announces Luc Montagnier and Robert Gallo's intent to collaborate on developing a vaccine against HIV/AIDS and briefly reviews their former rivalry.

Crewdson, John. "The Great AIDS Quest." *Chicago Tribune,* November 19, 1989.

This long article by Crewdson, a prizewinning Tribune *investigative reporter, strongly criticizes Robert Gallo's role in the discovery of the AIDS virus and suggests that Gallo may have been dishonest in claiming credit for some of the research.*

———. "Science Subverted in AIDS Dispute." *Chicago Tribune,* January 1, 1995.

In this follow-up article on the Robert Gallo investigation, Crewdson presents reasons for believing that Gallo made false statements about his laboratory's role in the discovery of HIV, even though the Office of Research Integrity dropped charges of scientific misconduct against him.

Gallo, Robert C. "The Early Years of HIV/AIDS." *Science* 298 (November 29, 2002): 1,728–1,730.

Gallo presents his version of the events that led up to the discovery of HIV in the early 1980s and demonstration that this virus causes AIDS.

———, et al. "Frequent Detection and Isolation of Cytopathic Retroviruses (HTLV-III) from Patients with AIDS and at Risk for AIDS." *Science* 224 (May 4, 1984): 500–503.

One of several articles in which members of Robert Gallo's laboratory describe their isolation of the virus that they believe to be the cause of AIDS.

Gorman, Christine. "Victory at Last for a Besieged Virus Hunter." *Time* 142 (November 22, 1993): 61.

Brief article describes Robert Gallo's feeling of being "completely vindicated" after the Office of Research Integrity dropped scientific misconduct charges against him.

Gottlieb, Michael. "*Pneumocystis* Pneumonia—Los Angeles." *Morbidity and Mortality Weekly Report* 30 (June 5, 1981): 250–252.

This description of an unusual form of pneumonia in five men is the first scientific report of the illness that later became known as AIDS.

Guo, H., et al. "Nucleotide Sequence Analysis of the Original Isolate of HIV-1." *Nature* 349 (February 28, 1991): 745.

This paper by scientists in Robert Gallo's laboratory states that the base sequence of the virus that Luc Montagnier brought to the Gallo laboratory in July 1983 does not match the sequence that Simon Wain-Hobson, a member of Montagnier's research team, published for LAV-Bru in January 1985—the sequence that had been shown to match almost completely the sequence of Gallo's HTLV-3B. Discovery of this discrepancy led to the discovery that a different strain of the French virus (LAV-Lai) had contaminated both the later Montagnier and the Gallo cultures.

Hilts, Philip J. "U.S. Drops Misconduct Case Against an AIDS Researcher." *New York Times*, November 13, 1993.

News article explains why the Office of Research Integrity, a government investigative agency, dropped charges of scientific misconduct against Robert Gallo after an appeals board reversed misconduct charges against Mikulas Popovic, a former member of Gallo's laboratory.

Marchione, Marilynn. "In a Surprise, HIV Infection Is Prevented." *San Francisco Chronicle*, September 24, 2009, pp. A1, A5.

Describes the results of a large human trial of a combination of two AIDS vaccines in Thailand, which showed that the combined vaccines reduced the risk of HIV infection by more than 31 percent.

Montagnier, Luc. "A History of HIV Discovery." *Science* 298 (November 29, 2002): 1,727–1,728.

Montagnier presents his version of the events that led up to the discovery of HIV in the early 1980s and demonstration that this virus causes AIDS.

———. "The Next Steps to Take in Beating AIDS." *Wall Street Journal*, October 21, 2008.

Montagnier tells why he believes that the HIV/AIDS epidemic can best be controlled by a therapeutic vaccine (one given after infection).

Norman, Colin. "A New Twist in AIDS Patent Fight." *Science* 232 (April 18, 1986): 308–309.

News article describes Robert Gallo's admission that a photograph in an earlier Science *article purporting to show Gallo's candidate AIDS virus, HTLV-3, in fact showed LAV, the candidate virus discovered by Luc Montagnier's laboratory. Norman says the admission is "likely to raise a few eyebrows"* and might have implications for the then-ongoing dispute over patent rights to the AIDS blood test.

Palca, Joseph. "Gallo Concedes Contamination (Again)." *Science* 252 (June 7, 1991): 1,369.
Brief news article reports Robert Gallo's admission in Nature *that the virus on which his laboratory based its blood test for AIDS, HTLV-3B, was actually a virus first discovered in Luc Montagnier's laboratory at the Pasteur Institute, which had contaminated the cultures in Gallo's laboratory.*

———. "The True Source of HIV?" *Science* 252 (May 10, 1991): 771.
Article describes the surprise discovery that LAV-Lai, a strain of HIV first isolated in Luc Montagnier's laboratory, first overgrew cultures of other HIV strains in that laboratory and then was unknowingly passed to the laboratory of Robert Gallo, where it contaminated that laboratory's virus cultures as well.

Poiesz, Bernard J., et al. "Detection and Isolation of Type C Retrovirus Particles from Fresh and Cultured Lymphocytes of a Patient with Cutaneous T-Cell Lymphoma." *Proceedings of the National Academy of Sciences* 77 (December 1980): 7,415–7,419.
In this article, Robert Gallo and his coworkers announce their isolation of HTLV-1, the first retrovirus proven to cause cancer in humans.

Popovic, M., et al. "Detection, Isolation, and Continuous Production of Cytopathic Retroviruses (HTLV-III) from Patients with AIDS and pre-AIDS." *Science* 224 (May 4, 1984): 497–500.
In this paper, Mikulas Popovic and his coworkers, members of Gallo's laboratory, announce that they have established a retrovirus, which they believe to be the cause of AIDS, in a continuous culture of T cells. The accuracy of some statements in the paper was later questioned.

Rosenthal, Elisabeth. "Top French AIDS Specialist Will Move to Queens College." *New York Times,* April 25, 1997.
Announces that Luc Montagnier is planning to join the faculty of Queens College, part of the City University of New York, where a new AIDS research institute will be built for him.

Sarngadharan, M.G., et al. "Antibodies Reactive with Human T-lymphotropic Retroviruses (HTLV-III) in the Serum of Patients with AIDS." *Science* 224 (May 4, 1984): 506–508.

In this paper, members of Gallo's laboratory report that the blood of a high percentage of AIDS patients contains antibodies that react with the retrovirus that the laboratory has discovered, providing strong evidence that this virus causes AIDS.

Shen-Yung, P., et al. "The Origin of HIV-1 Isolate HTLV-IIIB." *Nature* 363 (June 3, 1993): 466–469.

This paper by scientists at Roche Diagnostic Systems, a California subsidiary of the large Swiss pharmaceutical company Hoffman-La Roche, reports on genetic tests made with a new technique called PCR (polymerase chain reaction), which simplifies the analysis and comparison of small amounts of DNA. The Roche researchers state that MOV, one of the virus isolates in Gallo's laboratory that contributed to the pool from which HTLV-3B emerged, is genetically identical to LAV-Lai, a virus from Montagnier's laboratory.

Tahi, Djamel. "Interview Luc Montagnier: Did Luc Montagnier Discover HIV?" *Continuum,* winter 1997. Also available online. URL: http://www.virusmyth.com/aid/hiv/dinterviewlm.htm. Accessed November 2, 2010.

Interview published on an AIDS denialist site, in which the interviewer questions Montagnier extensively about whether Montagnier truly isolated the virus claimed to be the cause of AIDS and why he believes that the virus causes the disease. Montagnier maintains that he did isolate the virus and that it does cause AIDS.

Wain-Hobson, Simon, et al. "LAV Revisited: Origins of the Early HIV-1 Isolates from Institut Pasteur." *Science* 252 (May 17, 1991): 961–965.

Scientific article presents genetic sequence information revealing that a HIV strain called Lai contaminated other cultures in Luc Montagnier's laboratory in late summer 1983 without the researchers' knowledge and suggests that this strain may have contaminated cultures in Robert Gallo's laboratory as well.

Index